HOME REMODELING PITFALLS
AND HOW TO AVOID THEM

Duncan C. Stiph

Oct One. 1994

26 Judson Cone.
Woodbury CT 06798
266-4009

Home Remodeling Pitfalls and How to Avoid Them

The *definitive and comprehensive guide to successful home remodeling projects!*

by Duncan Calder Stephens

The
Globe
Pequot
press

Old Saybrook, Connecticut

Library of Congress Cataloging-in-Publication Data

Stephens, Duncan Calder.
    Home remodeling pitfalls and how to avoid them : the definitive and comprehensive guide to successful home remodeling! / by Duncan Calder Stephens. — 1st ed.

        p.   cm.
    Includes index.
    ISBN 1-56440-063-8 (pbk.)
    1. Dwellings—Remodeling.   I. Title.
TH4816.S745   1993
643'.7—dc20   92-41045
                                                                      CIP

Manufactured in the United States of America
First Edition/First Printing

Contents

Acknowledgments

It is fairly common for an author to say, "This book would have been impossible to write without the help of the following people. . . ." He then goes on to acknowledge and thank his wife, children, typist, proofreader, golfing buddies, and pet gerbils.

I too have a long list of people to whom I am indebted, not just for their support and inspiration, but because their help was an essential part of the project. These are the homeowners, contractors, builders, bankers, architects, and subcontractors who shared their experiences and hard-won remodeling knowledge with me in long, often eloquently humorous, entertaining, and informative interviews. Here they are, more or less in the order in which I met with them:

Howard Romaro, Design/Builder, Vermont
Mark Woodward, Builder, Vermont
Heather Marks, Homeowner, Vermont
John Rahin, Architect of Black River Design, Vermont
Mark Alvarez, Homeowner, Connecticut
Susan and Gus Southworth, Homeowners, Connecticut
Debby Watson, Homeowner, Connecticut
Susan Sobilinski, Inn Owner, Connecticut
David and Katie Heim, Homeowners, Pennsylvania and NYC
Michael DiZenno, Former Contractor, Connecticut
Jerron Baysinger, Contractor, Connecticut
Frank Husband, Remodeler, Connecticut
Theodore Ceraldi, Architect, New York
Lore and Ron Basil, Homeowners, New Jersey
Mark and Chris Ahasic, Brownstone Owners, NYC
Stephen J. Sweeney, Homeowner, Connecticut
Lydia Straus-Edwards, Architect, Connecticut
Robert Hanbury, Design/Remodeler, Connecticut
Liz Strasser, Homeowner, New York
Hal Wright, Homeowner, Maine
Jim Clark, Banker, Connecticut
Carol Bacon, Banker/Homeowner, Connecticut
Michael Walsh, Banker, Connecticut
Bret Zuraitis, Design/Remodeler, Connecticut
NAHB Remodelers Council, Washington, D.C.
National Association of the Remodeling Industry (NARI), Arlington, Virginia
American Institute of Architects (AIA), New Haven, CT Office

And the many friends and strangers who, once the subject of remodeling came up, contributed brief stories and insights on what they had learned during their remodeling process.

I certainly have to include Randy Crump and his crew, the remodelers on our project; my wife Eileen, who suffered through both the remodeling and book writing experience with me; and Betsy Amster, who edited my work and makes me wonder if maybe she should be listed as coauthor.

Thank you all. I hope the results make you feel your time was well spent and that you get some gratification from knowing others may be able to avoid a few of the mistakes you had to live with.

Introduction

A few years ago, when my wife and I were courting, we made two brave decisions. The first was to marry. The second was to renovate her little house completely so that it would fit the two of us and the life-style we anticipated. We thought it would be fairly simple: How hard could it be to turn a 750-square-foot two-bedroom ranch into a 1,600-square-foot Cape Cod?

Well, ten months and $85,000 later, we discovered it was a lot more complicated than we had thought. Fortunately, it was worth all the trouble. Where we once had four rooms and a bath, we now have six rooms and two baths, and where we once squeezed to seat four at dinner, we easily accommodated fourteen last Thanksgiving. Where we once set up folding chairs in the backyard to view the pond and sunsets, we can now see them both from the new deck and from inside the house. And the early-morning view from the huge new windows in our kitchen is a great way to start the day.

It probably doesn't surprise you to hear that remodeling our house was not a completely joyful experience. Meeting the requirements of the local Historical Commission added two months to the start date; so instead of taking advantage of an unseasonably warm November, the builders took the roof off during a very seasonable January. The carpenter, in an effort to make room for me in the shower, raised the roof peak an extra 4 feet without checking with us or the contractor. One of the crew moved into the house with a cot and his dog. He said he was protecting the tools, but we learned later he had broken up with his girlfriend.

Our experiences, good and bad, over the ten months of planning and building gave me the idea for this book. My wife, Eileen, and I learned the hard way that remodeling takes longer and costs more than expected. We are still paying off a personal loan we had to take out because the banker miscalculated the amount we needed. We survived what to me seemed endless hours spent in showrooms looking at carpeting, tile, fixtures, paint, furniture, and fabrics. And we eventually adjusted to the realization that we have different tastes. I also learned that what the builder and I thought were refinements, Eileen considered necessities. He and I thought the new snap-in mullions in the original picture windows in the old living room looked just like divided panes and were fine—we were wrong. My wife wanted the genuine article, which added a couple of thousand dollars to the cost.

Completing a remodeling project, I've learned, is like joining a secret fraternity whose members, when they learn that you can appreciate their problems, open up and share their experiences and frustrations with you. Unfortunately, all this highly useful information came to us *after* we needed it. Like most other people who have remodeled a home, we learned by the end that if we were to take on another remodeling project, we would do it entirely differently. In fact, all of the homeowners I interviewed in the course of writing this book felt exactly the same way. When I asked them if they would do things differently if they were to do them again, the answer was invariably yes. When I asked them if they'd be willing to tackle another remodeling job, the answer was often an emphatic *no*.

"If I had known what I know now, I could have saved a bundle of money and weeks of frustration," one homeowner moaned. He went on to tell me about the trouble he created when he accepted the lowest bid for a new roof and had to go back to another contractor when the low bidder ran out of money and quit the job. Other homeowners I interviewed were just as generous with their hard-earned experiences. One man didn't know about getting lien wavers (see chapter 2) and had to pay for his job twice, once to his contractor and the second time to the subcontractors and suppliers the contractor failed to pay. Another couple learned that if cleanup isn't specified in the contract, plumbers and electricians will refuse to patch the holes they make or otherwise clean up after themselves (see chapter 4).

Using a basic questionnaire as a guide, I asked these homeowners and dozens of others just like them what went wrong during their remodeling projects, how they solved the problems, and what they would do to avoid these problems if they had the project to do over again. I also asked what they learned or devised during the remodeling experience that reduced costs, time, or mental distress. To include the professional's point of view, I interviewed dozens of contractors, architects, builders, and designers as well. The result is a gold mine of good ideas and approaches, often in my interviewee's own words, covering everything from evaluating a contractor's proposal to maintaining your sanity when your kitchen is out of commission for months. If you read this book carefully, you'll know enough about remodeling pitfalls and how to avoid them to approach your first remodeling project as if it were your second.

Why Remodel?

People remodel and add on to their homes for as many reasons as there are people and homes. Perhaps you need to create additional space for a growing family and you've discovered that the "starter home" you moved into a decade ago with the intention of moving on when babies came along is now worth a bundle. Rising real estate values during that same period have made a move-up next house unreachable, so you decide to remodel and add to the investment you already have.

Or maybe your older home just doesn't work with today's casual life-style—it has a formal dining room you never use but no family room, or there's no bathroom downstairs. Then again, you may be hoping to increase the potential sales value of your house by modernizing the kitchen or adding a bath. Or perhaps you're interested in remodeling simply because you want a nicer kitchen or a more glamorous bath and you can afford it.

One architect told me that in his experience, people often remodel because someone has left them some money or because they are earning more and have the money to spend. They want to adapt their kitchen for entertaining or add a library and sun room to wile away their leisure hours.

Chances are you recognize yourself in one of these categories. But whichever category you fall into, be aware that before you scramble your first egg in your new kitchen, take your first soak in your new whirlpool tub, or curl up for the first time in front of the TV in your new family room, you are going to put yourself, your spouse (if you are married), and your kids and pets (if you have them) through one of the most frustrating, exasperating, costly, and confusing experiences most people will ever encounter.

The frustration and stress arise for several reasons. First, remodeling projects take a long time to get underway. The process begins with vague stirrings of discontent with your house that can go on for months or even years, but once you decide to do something about it, impatience grows as you begin to picture how much nicer your remodeled house will be. Second, remodeling involves *de*struction as well as *con*struction. When you build a new house, you start with nothing and gradually create something. But when you remodel, you start with something, destroy all or part of it, and only then begin to create something. The destruction phase is a difficult period for most homeowners.

Remodeling is also a little like traveling in a foreign country without knowing the language. Contractors don't talk about walls; they talk about top plates, bottom plates, studs, weight bearing beams, and headers. They don't talk about windows; they talk about double hung, casement, snap-in grille, true divided panes, eight-over-twelves, muttins, and mullions. Plumbers don't talk about toilets and sinks; they talk about vanities, lavatories, water closets, vents, and waste pipes.

Communication can become a major problem unless you learn a whole new language— several, in fact. In the initial phases everyone may seem to be speaking English, but when you begin to read your builder's proposal and the list of specifications (a list you have to authorize, mind you), you'll realize that the project has been translated into constructionese. The cabinet unit you want in your kitchen is now a 36 LS—or is it? The windows have become code numbers, your appliances are now model numbers, the insulation is in R-factors, and the floor has become 2 x10s 16" OC with ½" CDX underlayment. So you sign with the knowledge that if there is a discrepancy between what you hope you're getting and the code numbers, the code numbers represent what you will get.

Now that you are firmly in a shaky frame of mind, shut off the water, move the stove and refrigerator into the living room, cover everything with a fine coat of plaster dust, and you have all the ingredients for a stressful situation. Welcome to the wonderful world of remodeling.

Remodeling 101

Some homeowners approach the organization of a remodeling project the way I take on a new computer program. I read just enough of the instruction manual to begin, get in up to my neck, then find an expert to get me out of the mess I've made. If you're that type, slow down a second and read this quick review of the steps—and the cast of characters—involved in a remodeling project.

The Steps	Who
1. The Dreaming Phase	
Mulling and dreaming	You
Collecting information/clipping pictures	You
Recognition of need/ability to pay	You
2. The Planning Phase	
Rough planning, making sketches,	You, general contractor
drawing floor plans	(GC), architect, designer
Selecting the final plan	You
Preparing working drawings	GC, architect, designer
Obtaining financing	You and your banker
Drawing up the specifications	You, GC, architect, designer
Getting estimates/competitive bids	Four different GCs
Drawing up a proposal/agreement/contract	GC
3. The Selection Phase (overlaps with the planning phase)	
Locating/Investigating/Interviewing potential	
contractors, architects, or designers	You
Selecting contractor	You
Accepting and signing GC's proposal	You
Writing the first check	You
4. The Construction Phase	
Setting date to begin remodeling job	You and GC
Obtaining necessary permits	GC
Learning to live with construction	You and family
Making hundreds of selections/decisions	You and family
Learning to compromise	You and spouse
Learning how to handle problems and changes	You and GC
Writing more checks	You
Going over final problems to be corrected	You and GC
Writing last check	You
Enjoying your new, improved space	You and family

You Are Not Alone

Remember that you're not in this alone—architects, designers, contractors, lumberyards, and design specialty houses are all waiting in the wings to help you realize your remodeling project. In the following chapters you will learn whom to turn to for help at each stage. According to the homeowners I talked to, probably the most important decision you will make is the choice of an architect or general contractor (or both). In the next chapter you will learn what each of these professionals offers and how other homeowners have been able to make an informed choice between them. In subsequent chapters you will learn how to analyze and compare bids, how to read a contract, where to get financing, where all the money and time goes, what you can do to prepare for the builders, and, with the help of those homeowners who have gone before you, you will gain an appreciation of some of the problems you will encounter during construction.

This is your dream and your house, so you get to make the decisions. A *lot* of decisions. Many of them will be about things you didn't know you or your spouse had opinions about. In addition to preparing you for the chaos of construction, this book is intended to give you a good idea of the kind of decisions you'll confront and a little help in learning to compromise. As you read through it, you'll begin to understand what causes costs to go up and completion dates to be postponed, and you will learn how to anticipate and possibly to avoid problems. And in the (likely) event that you, your contractor, and the suppliers are not perfect, you will learn what to do when things go wrong.

If I have scared you a tiny bit with this introduction, good. You're already ahead of the game. Many homeowners believe that a rapidly declining bank balance is the only inconvenience they'll suffer during a remodel. Not so. In fact, your life is likely to be turned upside down for weeks, if not months. Fortunately, reading this book can help by allowing you to learn from other people's experience and mistakes.

CHAPTER
1

Planning

Architects call it "creating the client's program," but to the rest of us it's known as planning.
The process requires us to delve into our own likes, our dislikes, and our budget to determine
what it is we really need and want in a remodel—and what we can afford. It also requires us to
anticipate our future needs and problems. In this chapter you'll learn everything you need to
come up with a plan of action and even how to draw rudimentary floor plans. There's also a
detailed questionnaire at the end of the chapter to help you assess your needs and wants.

Whether you put a new bow window in the living room or, as we did, tear off the roof
and add another floor, it's still called remodeling. The amount of planning you need to do will
obviously depend on the scope of your remodeling project. Adding a deck off the back or side
of your house, for example, is a fairly simple remodeling project that offers a great deal of plea-
sure. But even for this comparatively simple project, you need to plan. Start by asking yourself
some serious questions: How big should your deck be? Where should it be located? What will
the local zoning laws let you build? Should it have multiple levels and planters? Do you need
help with the design? If so, where can you go for help? How do you find someone to build it?
How do you know the builder will do a good job and not rip you off? How much will it cost?
How long will it take?

Or perhaps you want to convert a closet under the stairs into a half bath. Not a huge project, but now you must ask some new questions: Will a half bath fit in the space? Can you get

plumbing into and out of the space? Will you need building permits? Is the local building inspector going to have to okay the job? How much do bathroom fixtures cost? Will the existing floor support the extra weight? How many different people will have to work on this job? Where will you find them? How much of a disruption will it be to the household? Can you draw the plans?

Then again, you may have your heart set on adding an entire master suite to the house. Now you are getting into the realm of major remodeling and construction, and the questions you have to ask are harder to answer without help: What will the addition look like when it's built? How can you make sure it will blend in with the original house? Will the existing furnace be able to handle the additional load? How will the traffic flow be affected? How fancy a bathroom do you want? How big should the closets be? Do you want carpeting or wood floors? What kind of windows do you want? If you're adding on to the master suite at ground level, do you want a full basement under it or just a crawl space? How will you use the space that used to be your bedroom? How much is all this going to cost?

If you're married or a single parent with children, the planning process becomes slightly more complicated because at least two people's likes, dislikes, and feelings must be taken into account (see chapter 11). Don't count on being able to predict the things your spouse loves or hates without asking. Many of our design prejudices are unconscious, and some of the conscious ones are kept quiet for the sake of harmony. Compromises are going to have to be made, and, unlike the solution to the annual vacation debate over the seashore versus the mountains, you can't have a picture window one year and divided panes the next.

You can't even use your present house as a measure of your spouse's likes and dislikes because most people accept what comes with a house when they buy it. But when you remodel you get the chance to make choices and satisfy dreams. As you make your choices and discuss your dreams, you may find that the husband or wife you thought you knew has a whole array of stubborn opinions—and a backbone you didn't know existed.

Your challenge during this early phase of your project is to be able to articulate those dreams. If you're clear about what each of you wants—a space where you can work free from the distractions of family life, a kitchen where you can cook and watch the baby play, a closet that will hold all your clothes—your architect or contractor will find it much easier to help you realize your vision.

Priming Your Creative Pump

Most remodeling projects are evolutionary rather than revolutionary—that is, they begin with twinges of dissatisfaction with your house in its present state. The twinge may be one of envy after you view a friend's recent renovation, or it could be the very real twinge you feel in your back as you lug the laundry up from the basement for the third time in a day.

If you know you want something else but you're not sure what, now is the time to clip pictures, plans, and suggestions out of magazines and newspapers. For years before we began our own remodeling job, my wife collected reams of clippings from the shelter magazines like *House Beautiful, House and Garden,* and *Colonial Homes.* She even organized them into folders labeled *windows, living rooms, kitchens,* and *baths.* She had obviously been planning for a remodeling project all her life.

Clip pictures you don't like as well as those you do. Both will come in handy once you have chosen an architect or contractor. While the contractor we eventually hired quailed at the sight of Eileen's piles of clippings (he was worried that he'd have to go into his "killer of dreams and breaker of hearts role" when he told us how much our dream was going to cost), we still found it useful to show him our files. Instead of groping for words ("We want something light-filled, airy, and open"), we were able to show him pictures of what we wanted. You'll notice I say what *we* wanted: Before we brought in the contractor, Eileen and I went through her files together and narrowed them down. We were fortunate that a woman born in Brooklyn and a man from the Midwest both preferred the New England look. If one of you likes stark modern and the other likes English cottage, you have some work to do before you call anyone to bid on the job. If you're deadlocked, consider consulting an architect or contractor, because many of them are experienced in filling the role of referee.

Exploring Your Wants and Needs

Once we agreed on the look we were after, we sat down to figure out what activities we wanted to pursue in our new space. Eileen wanted a place to read quietly, alone. I needed an office or a den where I could work or retreat. We also needed a bigger bedroom because my six-foot-six frame did not fit comfortably into any room in the existing house. We were pretty sure we would want to have overnight guests, especially my five grown children. We knew we'd entertain a fair amount. Extra bedrooms and a larger kitchen with room for a bigger dining table were therefore in order. So was a gathering place larger than the tiny living room, where we could watch TV or have family gatherings. We wanted our house to meet all those needs.

This process of exploring your wants and needs is crucial. If you hire an architect (see chapter 2), he or she will probably walk you through it. But if you want to get a head start, consult the list of questions I've provided at the end of this chapter.

Eileen and I made sure we discussed how we wanted to live, where the best views were, that the kitchen should be part of the family room, and that the shower heads should be extra high. As we debated the relative merits of different approaches, we tied them into short- and long-range options. For example, we both agreed that putting a shower in the downstairs bath would let us turn my office into a private area for an aging parent if the need arose.

This discovery phase of planning can go on for months, even years. (Of course, with some busy folks, it can take place over the weekend.) Most homeowners I talked with re-searched their planned remodel thoroughly over a period of time. The nature of their research varied. Some looked closely at friends' houses that appealed to them and tried to define what it was they liked. Others studied houses in shelter magazines like *Home* and *House Beautiful* and pored over detailed layouts in special house-plan magazines sold at bookstores. Everyone dreamed about what it was they wanted in a house. Nearly everyone made lists of what they wanted and needed both in the immediate future and in later years.

Architect: *I find in 75 percent of the cases that there is no planning beforehand. It is a decision that is made and acted upon within two or three months.*

Contractor: *How long do people spend on the plan? People I've worked with have spent two to five years. Very seldom less. That includes the thinking time.*

Putting Your Dreams Down on Paper

Contractor: *I would advise anyone contemplating a remodeling project to get in touch with real-ity by finding out the average cost per square foot for construction in their area and then drawing some floor plans to scale and seeing what fits.*

I've had people tell me they want to add a six-by-twelve-foot room to the back of their house. They want a laundry room in it, a half bath, and while we're at it some additional storage space and finally a small workshop. They haven't stopped to think that they can't fit all that into one six-by-twelve room. They really ought to sit down and write a wish list, then a list of their real needs, and finally a third list of what they can afford.

Floor plans can be enormously helpful in making you focus and in giving guidance to a contractor or an architect. If you can draw a straight line with a ruler and can grasp the con-cept that one square on a sheet of ¼-inch graph paper equals 1 foot by 1 foot of space, you're qualified to draw your own simple plans.

Begin by going to your local art-supply store and picking up a pad of ¼-inch graph paper and a triangular architect's ruler that will let you measure feet and inches without having to count squares. Also pick up an inexpensive T square and a small triangle. These will make drawing horizontal and vertical lines easy. You'll need a selection of both hard and soft lead pencils, too, the former to use while you're being creative and the latter for when you start getting down to details. And don't forget a good eraser.

Drawing floor plans without consideration for the size of the fixtures and the furniture that will end up in the rooms is an exercise in futility. So, while you're at the art store, ask to see the ¼-inch scale Furniture Indicator and the House Plan and Plumbing inking templates made by Picket. These green plastic sheets with ¼-inch scale die cuts let you trace everything from sofas, tables, beds, toilets, sinks, and kitchen appliances to bi-fold doors and even a grand piano. These features will look good in your drawings and will keep you from trying to shoehorn a 5-foot bathtub into a 4-foot bathroom.

The next step is to do what Eileen and I did: Measure your house and draw the existing plan on ¼-inch graph paper. I measured the inside and outside dimensions of the original house, noting the room sizes on a rough outline. Don't use a sewing tape measure for this operation; instead, get at least a 25-foot retractable ruler, preferably a ¾-inch-wide one that you can push along without it bending. Obviously, if you're only remodeling one room or installing a bath, you don't have to measure your whole house, but at the very least you should be aware of what's beside, under, and over the area you're planning to work on. For instance, your new toilet will require a vent stack that has to go all the way up through the roof. (Blending a 4-inch black PVC pipe into the decorative motif of the master bedroom can be a real challenge to a decorator!)

Once you have all the dimensions, get a fresh piece of graph paper and translate your rough drawing to scale. Your goal is to draw up a plan of the shell of the space you want to work with. We made a dozen photocopies of our basic floor plan so we wouldn't have to keep drawing the same thing over and over. I have since learned that architects use layers of tracing paper over the original drawing to make rough sketches of various layouts with those soft lead pencils.

Drawing floor plans is the least expensive part of remodeling, so don't hold back. There are, however, some cost considerations to keep in mind. It's best to leave the fireplace and chimney where they are and to try to stay within the original walls of your house. You can make one room out of two or three, or two or three out of one, add baths, and redesign kitchens with relative ease, but once you start adding rooms, ells, and foundations to the outside of the house or dormers and second stories on top, you are getting into a whole new range of complications and costs. Don't hesitate to do these things if you need the space, but start by trying to make creative use of the space within your existing four walls first. I think you'll find the process fascinating. Think of it as doing a jigsaw puzzle in which the only pieces you have are the border. You get to complete the center of the puzzle anyway you want, as long as it all fits.

Discussing every line or option before drawing it got to be too constraining, so Eileen and I broke into two independent design camps. She worked in the early mornings, and I seemed to hit my stride late at night. We came up with some pretty creative ideas for gaining a larger master bedroom, a new and larger kitchen, a second bath, an office for me, and even a third bedroom.

You can get more detailed and exact when you have gotten the knack of drawing floor plans and when you have narrowed down your options to two or three. Even then, remember that your drawings are for information only—they're not the official working drawings for your contractor, which will specify construction details like the sizes and grades of lumber. Leave the creation of these drawings to your designer, architect, or builder. Then he or she will be responsible for their accuracy, not you.

Contractor: *If you can't draw a straight line with a ruler, get one of those home-planner kits. Stanley has one, and many of the decorating and building magazines offer them, too.*

If all this sounds too daunting, you can always buy a home planner kit at your local lumberyard or building-supply store.

Moving walls and furniture around using a home-planner kit may not make you feel wildly creative, but anything you can do to visualize your project will expedite the remodeling process. Those ready-made plans will also act as a starting point when you sit down with your contractor or architect.

Lay It Out So You Can See It

Since we had decided to go outside the original four walls and were working with a 100-by-150-foot lot, the size of our proposed addition was important, especially because we wanted to keep enough room outdoors to play bocci and croquet. In order to get a clear idea of the "footprint" of our new and improved house (the amount of land the house itself would occupy), we staked out the various options on the lawn and walked around in them. We even got up on a stepladder to see what the view from the new deck would be like. When we saw the outline in string on the grass, it became very apparent just how much land our original ideas ate up .

A California homeowner I interviewed had a similar problem: *We live on a steep hillside lot in southern California. When we realized how much of our back patio we'd have to sacrifice to an addition, and also how hard it would be to get heavy equipment back there to dig, we decided to add a room on top of the garage at the front of the house instead.*

This sort of walk-through works inside the house too, particularly if you are dividing a large space into smaller ones. Mark off your new rooms and walk around in them. You can even use this approach during your remodel. Once the shell of our new second floor was up, our builder drew chalk lines on the subflooring where all the walls and doors would be. We were able to make changes just by erasing chalk lines—and we did.

Homeowners: *We wanted to put a deck off the side of our house that would allow us to get to the side yard where the kids played without walking all the way around the house. We were going to put a bay window in the kitchen and some French doors off the living room to get to the deck. We walked through that mentally for many months, imagining traffic patterns. I wanted French doors because they look so neat, but I changed my mind when I measured the swing area of the doors and pictured putting furniture near them. It would have been a disaster. Then I suddenly realized it would be better to switch the bay window and the doors because of the traffic pattern. I was absolutely right.*

This couple was lucky. They kept playing with their design on paper and picturing it in the actual space until they got it right. A real benefit of this approach is that it will save you money by catching mistakes before they have been cast, if not in concrete, in wood and wallboard. Many people have to see a wall or a door in place before they realize it isn't right. Then they must either live with something that is less than perfect or tear it out and do it over. This is where cost overruns start (see chapter 6).

When and Where to Ask for Help

Remember as you work on your sketches and plans that this isn't a high school project where you must do all the work yourself or lose credit. If you run into a creativity block, ask for help. We did. After creating a dozen rough floor plans, we narrowed them down to the six shown on page 14. But we had no idea how many of the six were structurally possible or what the cost differences would be. Should we add a single-story addition off the back of the house or a second story over the garage at the side? A couple of the plans called for a two-story addition off the back. Our preference was for a second story on top of the original house, but we were afraid that going up instead of out would be much more expensive. So we called in three different contractors to get some expert help and ideas.

We sat with each contractor in turn around the tiny table in our tiny kitchen and presented our ideas. We had the good sense not to expect exact bids, but we hoped each contractor could give us general cost comparisons for the different options. Which of the options was the most expensive and which the least? What would the house look like with the addition? How much of the one-third-acre lot would it use?

The first two contractors had good ideas and some fairly far-ranging estimates of possible costs. They both said it would be impractical and very expensive to tear off the old roof and add a second story. (I thought we could just jack up the old roof and add walls. No one agreed with that theory.)

The plans we drew looked basically like this:

Rough Measurements
of Original House:

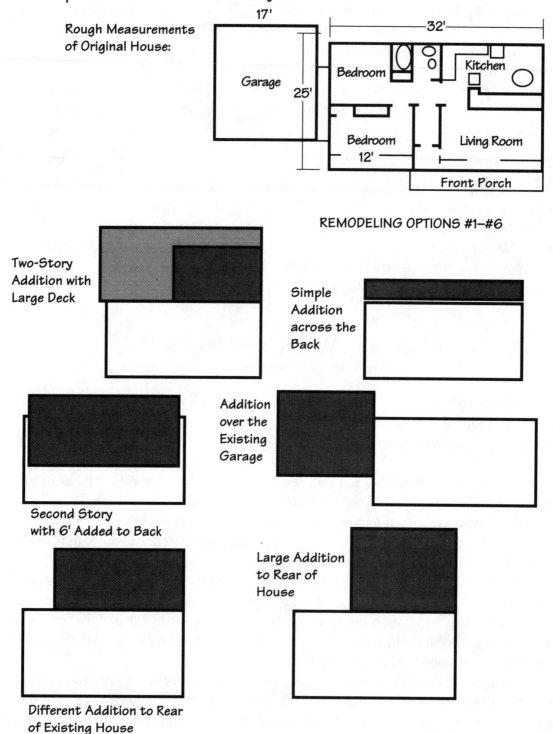

17'

Garage

25'

32'

Bedroom

Kitchen

Bedroom

Living Room

12'

Front Porch

REMODELING OPTIONS #1–#6

Two-Story
Addition with
Large Deck

Simple
Addition
across the
Back

Second Story
with 6' Added to Back

Addition
over the
Existing
Garage

Different Addition to Rear
of Existing House

Large Addition
to Rear of
House

Plot Plan and Elevation Drawings

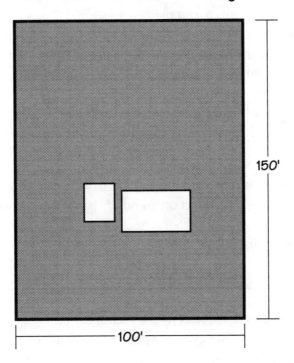

150'

100'

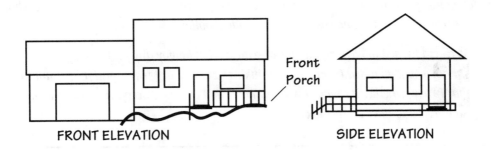

Front
Porch

FRONT ELEVATION   SIDE ELEVATION

The third contractor felt that adding a second story was the best option. He talked about retaining the basic shape of the house and lessening the footprint on the land and generally won our minds and hearts, especially when he showed us that the closet by the front door offered the perfect place to put the stairs.

Although none of the options we had drawn became the final plan, we shortened our contractor's design time because he knew most of the elements we thought were important just from reading our plans. Moreover, we could discuss his ideas intelligently because we had put so much thought into the details of our plans.

We were able to arrive at a very workable plan with his help, and you may be able to get a perfectly acceptable plan from your contractor, too. But keep in mind that there are other sources of design advice and help you may want to consider. To a large extent your choice depends on your budget and the complexity of your project.

Rent-an-architect

If you have painted yourself into a design corner with your efforts to create your own floor plans and are not comfortable turning your project over to a contractor before you know what you want to build, you can hire an architect on an hourly basis to review your plans and suggest alternative approaches to solving your problems. And you can then retain her to create the working plans. I don't think most people know about this type of service (we didn't), but it makes a lot of sense.

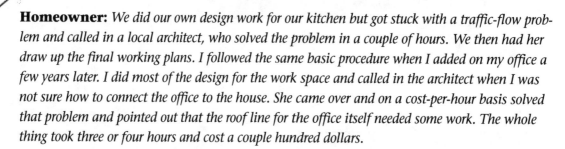

Homeowner: *We did our own design work for our kitchen but got stuck with a traffic-flow problem and called in a local architect, who solved the problem in a couple of hours. We then had her draw up the final working plans. I followed the same basic procedure when I added on my office a few years later. I did most of the design for the work space and called in the architect when I was not sure how to connect the office to the house. She came over and on a cost-per-hour basis solved that problem and pointed out that the roof line for the office itself needed some work. The whole thing took three or four hours and cost a couple hundred dollars.*

Homeowner: *I needed to have an architect because I don't enjoy any part of the creating process. I'm not a good planner. I don't enjoy thinking about what I want, and it isn't until it's finished that I know whether it's what I want or not. I don't care for decorating. I don't care for creating; so I needed to have an architect.*

I always assumed that architects wouldn't be interested in working on remodeling jobs in such a limited capacity or would charge an arm and a leg for their help. Not true. "Why wouldn't we agree to come in and be paid to do the part of architecture that is the most fun?" one architect responded when I questioned him.

Architect: *Many homeowners worry that architects will turn up their noses at small jobs, but usually that's not the case. Right now I'm working on a two-car garage on a difficult site that will cost about $22,000, a small kitchen renovation that will cost $3,000, and a new home that will cost over a million dollars. There's no project too big or two small for a small or medium-sized architectural office. Large firms are different: Though small projects aren't insulting, they're not inviting, either. They simply won't take them on.*

Local Lumberyards or Building-supply Stores

If your budget is tight and you are concerned that your plans might be bigger than your wallet, be aware that many local lumberyards or building-supply stores keep an estimator on staff who can give you an estimate of what your materials cost is likely to be, even from your rough floor plans. He will list the construction materials you will need and compile schedules, or lists of the numbers, styles, and sizes of windows and doors. Your lumberyard will probably not compile schedules for your plumbing or electrical needs, however. For these you will have to go to a plumbing-supply store and an electrical-supply store, respectively.

Of course, these estimates will not include the cost of a contractor and the labor costs for the various subcontractors, but the estimator may be able to give you a ballpark figure based on experience that will give you a pretty good idea of where you stand. While you're there you might ask for the names of some local contractors they recommend and thus get started on the next phase of your remodeling project: finding the people to do the work. In return for all their help, the people at the lumberyard will expect the opportunity to bid on the building supplies you will need, of course.

Companies Specializing in Kitchen and Bath Renovations

If a kitchen or bath remodel is on your mind, you might explore one or more of the many companies specializing in bath and kitchen renovations. Again, remember that these suppliers are in business to sell materials, fixtures, and sometimes construction services and will be nudging you toward the high end of their lines. They will also be bending your designs to fit their materials and standard sizes.

This is not a bad way to go if you don't require undue amounts of originality—and many of our houses couldn't stand it if we did. Moreover, kitchen and bath specialty shops usually have a good deal of experience. Many of them keep all the various subcontractors needed on the payroll and consequently have more control over scheduling than do general contractors and architects.

The design and consulting portion of the job is free. Since there is often room to negotiate prices, it is a good idea to solicit designs and bids from two or three such suppliers. Let each one know that you are getting bids from others. When it comes time to choose, make sure you are comparing bids for similar services and materials. (See chapter 3.)

Companies Specializing in Solar or Sun Rooms

If you want to add a single room to your house or even expand one, you might investigate the various solar or sun rooms available on the market. These lean-to–like structures are usually made of insulated glass on an aluminum or wood frame. They can be used to solve a design problem by extending a living room, dining room, or kitchen a few feet, or they can be built on an existing porch or deck. Standard sizes range in width from a couple of feet to more than 15 feet and in length from 8 to 20 feet in 4-foot sections. By utilizing solar heat or tapping into your existing house's heating system, they can be used year-round. Screened units are also available at less cost. They will give you additional room year-round in southern climates and during the summer months in the north.

Erecting a sun room can be less expensive than traditional construction, particularly if you already have a deck that will hold one. Most of the firms selling the units will also install them. The cost of a 5 by 16-foot curved roof, insulated-glass sun room with a sliding door and aluminum frame is about $6,500, according to one manufacturer's catalogue.

Carpenters and Other Craftspeople

A banker friend told me about an experience he had when he was building an addition to his house. He decided to do the job himself, even though he knew nothing about carpentry or any of the other trades he would need. When he got to the roof, he measured the angle and cut the roof rafters, but when he tried to nail them to the ridge rafter, they would slide down each time he hit the nail. He tried starting the rafter above the ridge and timing his hits so the rafter would be in line when the nail hit the ridge, but it didn't work.

In the middle of this his wife sent him to the supermarket and there, over his head as he started to go in, was a carpenter working on a small peaked roof, nailing rafters to the ridge board. He got the carpenter's attention and proceeded to explain his project at home and the problem he was having. The man stopped working, looked down at him, and asked, "Hasn't anyone ever told you how to handle that problem?"

"No", my friend responded. "How should I handle it?"

"Don't be so damn cheap. Hire a professional carpenter to do your work."

The carpenter had a point. I have been referring to architects and contractors as sources for plans and knowledge, but it is the carpenter who will do the actual work. Often a carpenter will handle the electrical or plumbing chores as well.

Don't overlook the possibility of a simple solution to your remodeling problems. We've been discussing planning for fairly elaborate projects, but maybe adding a bow window to the kitchen, taking out a wall between two small rooms, or tearing out the bathroom floor and replacing the sink with a new vanity will create the feel or space you need. Call in a carpenter to discuss the project. He or she has probably handled hundreds of situations like yours and will not only tell you how it can be done but may come with some creative ideas of his or her own. The carpenter will certainly take some measurements, call the local lumberyard for prices, and give you a quote. The next time you'll hear from him or her will be when he or she reports that your materials have come in and that work will begin the next morning.

Homeowner: *Our neighbor had a replacement-window firm change all the windows in her house to thermopanes. We had their salesman give us an estimate for our family room and kitchen. It came to over $10,000 so we narrowed it down to the kitchen and bathroom windows, and it still was a couple of thousand. On a friend's recommendation we called in a local carpenter. His estimate was in the hundreds, so we hired him. Two days later when we came home, we had new windows in both rooms, all the trim work matched the rest of house both inside and out, and he had even painted everything.*

I never had the heart to tell my neighbor how little we paid because she still has to hire a painter to paint her house because of all the new shingles that had to be installed around each window.

Much of this world's remodeling is done by local carpenters or builders who handle most of the work on a project themselves or with one or two helpers. They will only call in other tradespeople as they need them and are usually willing to let their clients shop for bargain materials and fixtures themselves. The whole project will probably be done quickly, on an informal basis, with a cost range rather than a bid, and at an hourly rate.

The fact that many carpenters can handle all the duties of a contractor should not be too surprising. After all, most contractors start as carpenters and only get away from actual hands-on building when they start juggling several jobs at the same time.

Finding a great local carpenter or builder is like finally locating a great mechanic for your car. You treasure him and keep going back for work year after year. If a carpenter or a builder is particularly popular, you may find your neighbor slightly reluctant to give out his name. Persist. He is worth finding, and if your remodeling job is within his scope (he will probably let you know if it isn't), give him strong consideration.

Design/Remodeling Firms

These firms are designed to fill the gap between architect-designed projects and those drawn on the back of an envelope by a carpenter. They provide conceptual drawings and estimates and will also build what they design if you hire them to go all the way. Relative newcomers to the home remodeling scene, they can be found through two associations: NARI (the National Association of the Remodeling Industry) and the NAHB (National Association of Homebuilders) Remodelers Council, a division of the National Home Builders Association. Each association qualifies the design/remodelers it certifies through a series of required courses. Check local listings or contact the national headquarters, listed in chapter 2.

Design/Remodeler: *While architects might come up with great plans, their pricing isn't as firm or accurate as ours is. When you take an architect's plans to market, you may find you've been designed beyond your budget. You stand the chance of spinning your wheels for a long time, whereas with a design/build or remodeling firm, you cut out that step. The first thing a design/ remodeler will ask is, "What is your budget?" Once we know, we make sure your design doesn't carry you beyond that point.*

The typical design/remodeling firm has an experienced draftsperson on staff—often the owner/builder himself or herself. Some firms have made the move to CAD (computer-aided design) systems to create everything from deck designs and kitchens to a complete house with the push of a few keys.

The firms I talked to treated the design and remodeling functions of the company as separate operations. The construction side was free to bid on projects originated by other designers, and the design arm was free to sell its services separately. In fact, it is not uncommon for the specifications and plans created by the designer to be sent out to other contracting firms for bid.

Design/Remodeler: *Many of our design clients send out our proposals to other contractors for bid because our proposals are the most complete description of the job. We treat each portion of our business separately and don't mind the competition. We do have an advantage in the bidding, however, because we know the job so well.*

A Planning Questionnaire

Often the success of planning depends on asking the right questions. The following questionnaire is intended to make you think about your home and how you live in it in a way you may never have thought about before. Go over it with your spouse and discuss your answers. You may learn a lot about yourself and each other, and your plan will be the better for it.

General Questions:

Since you are planning a renovation or addition, what are the major shortcomings of your existing house? Functional shortcomings? Aesthetic shortcomings?

_____

_____

_____

Principal use of the house? _____ First home _____ Second home

Is there a seasonal pattern? _____

_____

Do you have special interests or activities that need special spaces? _____

_____

_____

_____

Do you have a preference for or prejudice against:
_____ single-level, _____ multilevel, _____ multistory structures?

Do you have a size or square-foot number in mind? _____ sq.ft.

Do you have an approximate dollar budget for this project? $_____

Do you have an anticipated design and construction schedule?

Start date _____ Finish date _____

(Allow for design time and construction delays)

Do you have future plans for the house beyond this change? _____

_____

_____

_____

Site and Lot Questions:

Can you locate a site plan? _____

What do you like about your house site? _____

_____

_____

What are its drawbacks? (e.g., noisy road, future building next door)

_____

_____

_____

What direction does the prevailing wind come from? _____

What outdoor activities/spaces are important to you? (e.g., gardening, entertaining, relaxing, swimming in your pool, barbecuing, play area for kids, level area for sports: croquet, bocci, horseshoes, volleyball, etc.)

_____

_____

Do you enjoy, tolerate, or despise mowing the lawn and maintaining the grounds?

_____

_____

Car Questions:

How many vehicles do you have? _____

Where will they be stored? Garage? Outside? Covered? _____

Is the garage part of your remodeling plans? Is it new? Attached? Detatched? Are you eliminating garage for other use?

_____

_____

Storage Questions:

What equipment do you own? (e.g., riding mower, push or power mower, snow blower, rototiller, bicycles, boats)

_____

_____

_____

What else do you own that requires storage? (e.g., garden tools, garbage cans, outdoor furniture, grill, kids' toys, sports equipment [frightening isn't it?])

_____

_____

_____

Have you considered a freestanding shed? _____

Do you need space for a workshop? What will you do in your shop?

_____

_____

_____

Terrace, Deck, and Porch Questions:

Have you considered the following? (These are important elements of a house; they allow and encourage people to get outside. They all require surfaces that are flat and hard enough to be suitable for placing furniture. Depending on what part of the country you live in, they extend the outdoor season to varying degrees.)

☐ Terrace: concrete, flagstone, or brick pavers on grade.

☐ Deck: usually raised above adjoining ground and thus dryer.
  Usually needs railing.

☐ Covered porch: deck with roof; a great place to be on a warm rainy day.

☐ Screened-in porch: Keeps mosquitoes out, lets in some rain occasionally.

☐ Insulated, enclosed porch: becomes a sun room or greenhouse and is almost another room. It can be used year-round.

Which of the following activities do you want to provide outdoor space for? Eating? Kids playing? Entertaining?

_____

_____

_____

_____

Entrance Questions:

Is a formal entry hall important along with a functional entry? _____

Is a formal entry hall unnecessary but a front door important? _____

Could you get rid of a formal entry hall and try to make the functional entry suitable for guests?

_____

_____

How big a front closet do you need? _____

Will it be used for anything besides guests' coats?

_____

_____

_____

Does the everyday entry (mudroom) need a bench, shelving, hooks, boot storage, etc.?

_____

_____

_____

Basic-use Questions:

What do you want to be able to do in this house? (e.g., eat, sleep, relax, work, entertain)

What stage of life is your family in?

- ☐ Small house without kids - efficient, compact, entertaining.
- ☐ Kids - privacy, separate bedrooms.
- ☐ Getting old - fewer stairs, easier maintenance.

Eating Questions:

Range of possibilities: formal dining room, dining-table area out of kitchen, kitchen, breakfast nook, country kitchen, island or eating counter.

_____

_____

_____

_____

How separate or connected do you want the cooking and eating activities?

_____

_____

_____

_____

How often do you entertain? _____

How often does the whole family eat together? _____

Kitchen Questions:

(The kitchen is the social center of the house. Most people use it at least twice a day.)

Who does the food preparation? One or more people? How many at a time?

_____

_____

_____

How often do you do food shopping? Who does it? _____

How much food storage do you need? _____

_____

_____

When guests come over do they always end up in the kitchen? _____

Do you want them there? If not, stay out yourself and have everything done ahead of time or hire a chef. If you like the company, design a bigger kitchen and let them help, or build a small working kitchen with a peninsula or island for guests to sit at and watch without getting in your way.

_____

_____

Do you have any special requirements or unique kitchen habits?

_____

_____

_____

_____

Have you considered the work triangle and selected the appliances you want?

_____

_____

Everyday-living Questions:

(The traditional "living room" is often one of the least-used rooms in today's house.)

How do you want to live, relax, entertain, watch TV?

_____

_____

_____

Do you need one large room for entertaining?

_____

_____

What functions do you want to create separate areas for?

_____

_____

_____

_____

What functions do you want to combine? (e.g., entertaining, kids' playing, adults' TV watching, kids' TV watching, reading, listening to music, playing music, exercising)

_____

_____

_____

_____

What kind of work will you do at home? (e.g., pay bills, keep records, do office work, read, earn a living)

_____

_____

_____

_____

How will you accommodate these functions? (Your choices can include the use of a great room, keeping room, study, den, TV room, or family room.)

_____

_____

_____

_____

Sleeping Questions:

(Although most of the time that you're in the bedroom it's probably dark outside, daylight, sun, and views can be important considerations. The other things you do in your bedroom can influence its design.)

Have you considered using the bedroom as a sitting area, work area, exercise area, dressing area, or vanity area?

_____

_____

_____

How big a bedroom do you want? Big (over 12x12), average, or small?

_____

What are your storage needs? Walk-in closet(s), regular closet, or no closet but more space for wardrobes and dressers?

_____

_____

_____

Do you have a need for seasonal storage of clothing? If so, where should it be?

_____

_____

_____

Do you want a master bath off your bedroom?

_____

_____

_____

_____

Will your kids have separate bedrooms or share?

_____

_____

_____

Do you want them close to you or far away? _____

_____

_____

Do you expect your kids to spend time in their rooms playing, studying, etc. or in another location? (Remember to think ahead; they won't be this age for long.)

_____

_____

_____

Do you want or need a guest bedroom?

_____

_____

_____

Should it have a separate bath or will guests share a bath with the family?

_____

_____

_____

Can the guest room double as something else? (e.g., a den, TV room, or playroom)

_____

_____

_____

Bathroom Questions:

(Since the bathroom and kitchen are the two most frequently selected remodeling projects, here are some things you might consider. A bathroom doesn't have to be a traditional 5x8 combination of sink, toilet, and tub. Consider a separate toilet room. This is a European notion that can free up the rest of the bathroom facilities. Consider a separate tub and shower. Some people think soaking in a bathtub is a relaxing and enjoyable activity. Eliminating the need for a shower enclosure around the tub opens up the possibilities for a more pleasant space.)

Would you like double vanities (ideal for the family with conflicting morning schedules)?

_____

_____

_____

Is there a good scenic view possibility for placement of the toilet or tub?

_____

_____

Laundry Questions:

Who does the laundry? Mom? Dad? Kids? _____

Are you trying to do anything else at the same time? _____

_____

_____

Where do you want it? Basement with a chute? First level? Second floor? (Remember to consider the issues of noise and the inevitable flooding.)

_____

_____

Fireplace Questions:

(Fireplaces are a traditional focal point or heart of the house, though they're inefficient in comparison to a wood stove.)

Do you want a fireplace in your home? If so, in association with what activities?

_____

_____

_____

Might you consider a wood stove? If so, in association with what activities or functions?

_____

_____

_____

Have you considered the resupply and storage of wood?

_____

_____

_____

Solar Questions:

(Particularly in the north, it makes good sense to consider orienting some of your rooms and windows toward the sun to gain some active or passive solar heat as well as to brighten the interior.)

Which of the following rooms do you want sunlit, and when? Morning, all day, or afternoon? Kitchen, dining area, formal eating area, living and relaxing area, bedroom, work area, study, library, greenhouse, deck, kids' play area?

_____

_____

_____

Footnote: This list of questions was drawn from a questionnaire created by the architects of Black River Design, who assign it to their clients as homework for new houses and remodeling projects.

CHAPTER
2

Who's Going to
Be in Charge Here?

Finding and Evaluating Architects,
Contractors, and Other Professionals

Now that your planning process is well underway, you need to decide who is going to oversee your remodeling job: you, a contractor, an architect, a design/remodeler, or some combination of the above.

Traditionally, most homeowners go directly to a general contractor. That's the route we took, but I now realize, from many of the horror stories I've heard since, that we were fortunate in our selection. A good contractor can lead you through all the phases of a remodeling project, from helping you decide what to do and creating adequate working drawings to getting the work done. A bad contractor can lead you astray and cost you dearly in frustration and money.

For some remodeling jobs it makes sense to be your own general contractor: If you're getting your house repainted, replacing a roof, or dealing with a kitchen or bath remodeling specialty firm, for example, you can handle it on your own. The architects I talked to also believe that homeowners can handle almost any job that requires only one or two subcontractors, particularly if they have located a good carpenter with some crossover skills in plumbing and electrical work. But if your job is more complicated, there are compelling reasons *not* to act as your own general contractor, as you'll see below.

If your job involves major alterations to your home or requires creative problem-solving skills, consider retaining an architect. Architects can also be helpful if you have absolutely no idea what you should do or how or where to start. A builder can usually find a technical solution to a remodeling problem, but an architect may find a creative solution. Architects are trained to step back and look at the bigger picture, and, as I'll discuss below in more detail, they can also act as your watchdog on the job. Since they are never engaged in the actual construction, architects can plan several steps ahead and very possibly help you save time and avoid problems.

Design/remodelers are usually made up of the cream of the local construction crop. They are skilled builders who have the experience and have taken the necessary courses through NAHB or NARI to qualify as Certified Remodelers. They provide both the design skills to work with you on the plan and the organizational and construction skills to supervise the actual construction. Since they create the working drawings and also prepare the estimates and bids, they are in a good position to keep a project within a client's budget.

In the rest of this chapter you will learn in greater detail about the services and skills you can expect from these and other professionals available to oversee your job. You will also learn how to find them, how to evaluate them, and finally, how to select the best one(s) for you.

What a *Good General Contractor* Can Do for You

The general contractor or GC is the person who takes your remodeling project from lines on paper to a new three-dimensional space in your home—*if* you decide a GC is the person you want to oversee your job. How painless the process is for you will depend on how good your GC is.

The GC may or may not do any actual physical labor on your job, but that's not what you're paying him for. Our GC pounded nails during the framing process just to take out some frustration and tiled both bathrooms because he loved to do it. The rest of the time his job was to see that things got done correctly and in a timely manner.

Your first contact with a general contractor will probably be when you invite one to your home to meet you. During that visit he will get a general idea of the project you have in mind and decide whether he wants to bid on it. He may decide the job is too big for him or too small . . . or too confused. Since GCs are independent by nature, they can refuse a job or bid so high they won't get it. Many tell me they have learned there are some homeowners to be wary of, including lawyers, engineers, and those who have dust covers over all the furniture and a painted garage floor.

If you have a preconceived idea of what a contractor should look like, you're probably going to be in for a surprise. It's not unusual for a GC to show up in a coat and tie. Contractors are businesspeople, frequently college graduates, who may well handle more money in a month than you do in a year. A GC may also show up in a ponytail and bib overalls. Appearance is usually unimportant.

What You Should Get from Each General Contractor

All the contractors you invite to meet with you will discuss the project, make recommendations, and possibly submit bids. Once you have selected your contractor from among the bidders (see chapter 3), you can expect:

- a detailed list of what work is to be performed;
- a list of the materials needed by quantity or brand name;
- a list of the jobs your GC plans to subcontract;
- an estimate of the time the job will take. (Since all contractors have a short memory for disasters and tend to be optimists, the time estimate will be based on the assumption that everything will work smoothly for the first time in history. Don't send out the invitations to the house warming just yet.); and
- a starting date.

Other Responsibilities of the General Contractor

Your GC should also:

Obtain building permits. It is the GC's responsibility to get the various building permits required by your city or town. (Keep in mind that the person who applies for the permit is the one held responsible for compliance.) He should also outline any steps you must take yourself to get the job rolling. In our case our contractor alerted us to the fact that we needed to get the water company to shut off the water at the street because we were tearing off the roof in January and shutting off the heat.

Create a schedule. It is the GC's job to schedule all the work and the people to do it so there is as little downtime as possible. That's more complicated than it sounds, since many of the skilled tasks, such as electrical and plumbing work, can only be done after certain parts of the project are complete yet *must* be done before other parts, such as insulating and putting up the plasterboard, can start. Further complicating the situation is the fact that the subcontractors, or subs, will be working on other projects before and after yours which will have complications of their own.

Place orders. Your GC will be responsible for ordering all the materials and supplies for your project, seeing that they are delivered on time, and finding a safe, dry place to store them. Again, that's more complicated than it sounds. You really don't want the shower enclosure sitting on the front lawn for a month before the bathroom is ready. You also don't want the shower to arrive after all the walls and doors are installed, because you won't be able to get it in the house.

Schedule building inspectors. It is the GC's responsibility to arrange for the local building inspector and other officials to tour your project at the proper times. The number of inspectors will depend on local regulations and the scope of your job. We started with the health inspector, who checked our plans and then came back to actually look in the holes for our relocated septic system. The building inspector checked our electrical system and suggested a power upgrade and a new panel board as well as additional supports in the basement under the relocated supporting beam. The amount of lead time necessary for these inspections will vary from community to community. In our case the building inspector was only in town on Tuesdays and Thursdays but was readily available on those days.

Handle day-to-day problems. It is the GC's responsibility to keep the job moving. No matter how well thought out a project is in advance, unforeseen events will force him to modify the schedule. The sign of a good general contractor is how well he juggles these day-to-day emergencies and adjustments. Late deliveries and subs who don't show up are the two biggest causes of disruptions. A good GC will have inside work lined up if it rains and a series of tasks in mind that his crew can do if the roof shingles are the wrong color and have to be sent back.

Account for time and money. The GC is responsible for keeping track of the hours his crew puts in and the cost of materials that have been delivered, and for collecting the subs' bills. He is also responsible for presenting you with itemized bills, complete with backup invoices from suppliers, at the various stages of construction you have agreed upon. You're responsible for writing the checks.

Wrap everything up at the end. The GC's final responsibility is to see that all the little details on the *punch list* (a list you compile of things that have to be smoothed, fitted, attached, painted, and adjusted—see chapter 14) are completed and that you have a certificate of occupancy issued by your local building inspector. He should also provide you with mechanics' lien releases signed by all the subs and suppliers he has dealt with. These releases assure you that your GC has paid all the suppliers and subcontractors and that they have no further claim on your money or property. It is not uncommon for a contractor who is working too close to the financial edge to use the money coming in on one job to meet expenses on another. If something upsets his delicate balancing act and you don't have lien releases, you might have to pay all those bills again in order to keep your home.

Should You Be Your
Own General Contractor?

After reading the list above, you may be thinking, "I could do that." What could be so tough about making a few phone calls and a couple of trips to the lumberyard, ordering some fixtures, and supervising the subcontractors who will do all the actual work? Well, it's not quite that simple.

Contractor: *If you decide to be your own GC, you must be willing to accept the financial burden of mistakes. You have to be available hour by hour or even minute by minute to make decisions. If you have another job, don't think you can get away with being an absentee GC. You can't expect subcontractors to take on the responsibility and duties of a general contractor for free. The mason will always tell you what's best for him, not what's best for the plumber. I have seen plumbers try to put things in places where the GC has to say, "No way. You can't put it there because that is where my chimney has to go." Most homeowners simply aren't knowledgeable enough to do that.*

Contractor: *There's one way being your own GC might work: if you are willing to come home from work on a day-to-day basis and make decisions that have to be made. Even then I'm not sure. What happens when your plumbing sub asks you where you want to put the oil tank? If it's less than 10 feet from the circuit box, it's out of code. But that puts you 6 inches too close to the furnace or under the stairs or next to an exit door. A GC knows all this stuff. If he doesn't, it becomes his financial responsibility to correct the mistakes that are caused by his lack of knowledge.*

Architect: *Construction problems aren't usually the fault of a single subcontractor. Problems occur where different tradespeople come together—for example, the plumber and the kitchen-cabinet installer, the Sheetrocker and the electrician. If something goes wrong, each tradesperson will blame the other. When you have a GC, this sort of thing is his problem. He will either work it out with the subs or get someone else to fix it or do it himself. The homeowner GC doesn't have those options. He or she is caught in the middle.*

Other Points to Consider
if You Are to Be Your Own GC

Acting as your own GC is complicated. It has been said that an amphibious invasion is the most complicated project ever taken on by man. If that is true, construction must run a close second. Even if everything goes right—people show up when they say they will, materials and supplies are available and delivered on time, and the weather cooperates—you still have the task of planning what you want and when you want it.

Architect: *Being your own general contractor is a very dangerous thing. I am not even my own architect. I hired my associate to design my office and to oversee the construction even though it is in my own home. As a professional in the construction business, I have a high regard for the complexity of the business and each one of the trades.*

Acting as your own GC requires many skills. Here is a partial list of the subjects you must master, more or less in the order you will face them on a large project: planning; drafting; landplanning; conforming to zoning laws and local building codes; negotiating; financing; scheduling; surveying; hiring and firing; excavating; designing sewage or septic systems; pouring cement; supervising; making decisions; insulating; roofing; glazing; installing electrical fixtures, wiring, plumbing and heating, flooring; ordering cabinetry; building; carpeting; painting; decorating; bookkeeping (accounts payable—there are no receivables); solving problems; inspecting. You will also need imagination, energy, and infinite patience.

Acting as your own GC is not the quickest route. Even if you follow all the advice in this book, you will not necessarily shorten the construction time required for your project. But you will have a more realistic estimate of the time it will actually take. Our contractor met his crew on the site each morning at 7:00 A.M. (with coffee and doughnuts) to lay out the tasks for the day. After that his job was to keep them supplied with materials. He was the one who made the trips to the lumberyard for the Sheetrock screws and the dozen additional two-by-fours. He was the one who returned the wrong-color shingles, took the orders for sandwiches for lunch, and went and picked them up.

Those are tasks you might be expected to do if you are a do-it-yourself GC, plus a million more. You still have to visit all those showrooms and select windows, doors, hardware, lighting fixtures, carpeting, bathroom fixtures, kitchen cabinets, bathroom vanities, ceramic tile, paint, and dozens of other things.

Homeowner: *You might save some money by being your own GC, but you can't be in a big rush. If you schedule it too tight, there will always be delays that mess up your schedule. If a guy says it will take three days, assume it will take six days. Accept that there will be many days when nothing happens.*

Scheduling a major renovation can be a real bear when you act as your own GC. If you act as your own GC, don't expect to get a lot of cooperation from your subs. A general contractor may have the same problems, but generally he has a little more control over his subs because they rely on him for work. When he threatens them, they pay attention. When you threaten them, it may not have much effect. You have almost no leverage over them except money, and if they have had previous experience working for a homeowner GC, even your money may not be enough incentive for them to take you seriously.

Acting as your own GC is likely to cost you money. Subcontractors will give a professional GC a better price than they will offer you. Once they've worked with a few homeowners directly, they expect you to be a pain in the butt. They know you are going to cost them more time and money because of your inability to make snap decisions on the job. They are also afraid that when it comes time to get paid, they're going to have to sit down and justify each item on the bill and probably not get the last payment because you aren't grown up enough to accept the fact that you made the mistakes that cost additional time and material.

Builder: *As a subcontractor I would not work for a homeowner GC unless I was on a straight time-and-materials basis that guaranteed I would get paid for every hour I spent on the job whether I was building, waiting, or tearing something out. All the lumber and supplies would have to be paid for by the owner.*

The question you have to ask yourself is: "Will the 10 to 15 percent I am saving by being my own GC still be there at the end of the job?" If you earn $50,000 a year, your hourly wage for a forty-hour week is roughly $25. Good carpenters earn between $10 and $16 an hour. In most cases, then, you'd be better off working at your own job and hiring someone else to supervise the project.

Some people try to save some money by doing part of the actual work themselves. We told our contractor that we would do the interior painting on our job. Then I watched all the small-paned windows going in and suggested he line up some painters.

Minimizing the Risk of Acting as Your Own GC

You can be your own GC and make it work if you take a clear look at the scope of your project and take some precautions. The clear look should tell you how complicated the project is, how many different subtrades will be required, and how much disruption to your household will be involved. The precautions include:

- getting a good, clear set of working drawings for your project;
- doing a lot of advance planning and anticipating;
- lining up a backup expert like an architect or designer; and
- working within an undemanding time frame.

Homeowner: *I say be your own GC. I don't think it's too complicated if you have an architect's help in laying out the job logically and telling you who to bring in when.*

I would recommend that you retain an architect or designer to create a set of working drawings for your project and a list of materials so you can solicit comparable bids from your subs. It would then make a lot of sense to pay that architect to check your project a couple of times a week or as each phase is near completion to see that it has been done correctly. It will give you a little additional weight with your subs.

Architect: *I have had several experiences, both good and bad, in which the homeowner was his own GC. In one case the owner happened to be a plumber. He told me the budget he wanted to maintain, and I designed a small addition to his house. Since his budget was constrained, he wanted to do a lot of the work himself, including overseeing the project. I had no objection to that as long as my drawings were adhered to and all the building-code requirements followed.*

What a *Good* Architect Can Do for You

An architect can't take the place of a GC—after all, it's the GC who estimates the time and materials needed, submits the bid, and hires the subcontractors. But an architect *can* oversee your project alongside your GC. In that case the architect is representing you on the job site, solving problems as they arise, seeing that the subs' work is to specifications, and approving the invoices for your payment.

Americans seem reluctant to hire architects and apparently have been ever since we've been building houses. Eileen and I didn't even consider using an architect for our remodeling job. We didn't know any better, yet I've since learned that people in Europe and Africa use architects as commonly as Americans use accountants or attorneys.

That makes sense to me because a good architect offers a combination or blending of the artistic and the mechanical. His or her objective is to find a practical solution to a problem and, at the same time, to create a beautiful space that blends in with and matches the space around it. An architect's contribution can be as simple as a few hours of consulting time and rough sketches of a variety of creative floor plans and as involved as detailed working drawings and full supervision of the construction project.

There are advantages to using an architect beyond getting a good design solution. For one thing the cost of a professional architect or designer assisting you in a capital improvement to your home can be written off when you sell the property. There is some evidence that many banks also recognize the benefit of using an architect and are often more comfortable about approving a loan when you do use one.

When I talked to architects and designers, they were able to give me very persuasive arguments for using all or at least part of the services they offer:

An architect can keep you from making costly mistakes in construction (when you serve as your own GC) that the local building inspector could demand be removed. Of course, a good contractor should have this knowledge too.

Architect: *One of my clients, who was acting as his own general contractor to save money, hired a carpenter who was new to construction to frame the addition according to the plans I had prepared. However, in an effort to please, the carpenter overbuilt the house by doubling the size of the supporting members and caused structural problems. He also increased the heights of the windows.*

As the architect, I am responsible for making sure that the buildings for which I submit plans for approval to the local board comply with my drawings, whether I am overseeing the construction or not. Once I saw that the window heights had been increased, I was required by law to report that fact to the local authorities. The changes caused problems for all concerned, problems that were eventually worked out but that could have been avoided. By trying to save a couple of dollars, this particular client wound up spending much more.

An architect can help you solicit more businesslike bids. By hiring an architect to prepare the working drawings and specifications, you'll be in a position to offer each contractor bidding on your project the same information, which will allow you to compare the bids on an apples to apples basis.

An architect can help you review the bids you receive, interview the contractors, and advise you on selecting the best contractor for the job. If you are using your architect's plan, she will have a vested interest in your selecting a capable GC. She can also help you read and evaluate the contract you get from your contractor.

An architect can act as your watchdog on the job. Architects offer a range of construction services beyond design, including being on the job site as *clerk-of-the-works* (an old-fashioned term meaning *watchdog*) for at least a part of every day. If you wish, your architect will confer with your GC, help work out the scheduling of the subs, make on-the-spot decisions, solve problems, and generally act as your representative. Called *active management* of a project, this service may seem to poach on your GC's territory, but some contractors have told me they appreciate having another informed professional around to discuss ways of solving problems. It also tends to keep the homeowner out of the GC's hair.

When an architect actively manages a project, she usually signs off on the contractor's invoices. It is standard building practice to give a contractor 25 percent when you sign the contract, 25 percent when the job is half done, a chunk more when it's three-quarters done, and the remainder when the job is finished. You can check with the architect at each phase to see that the work is being done the way you expected it to be.

Of course, active management costs. Several homeowners I spoke with paid their arch-

Homeowner: *When you negotiate an architect's fee for design and active management, it should be based on a fixed amount or a percentage of the budgeted amount for the project. If you let his fee go up as costs increase, he has no incentive to keep costs down.*

tects 8 percent of the total remodeling cost for the design work and 3 percent additional for their supervisory help. Your architect will draw up a separate contract for services of this scope so you will know what she will provide and the fee before you start.

For less money, an architect can also provide smaller chunks of service called *supervision*, which involves checking out the job once or twice a week. In that case your architect will meet with you alone or with you and your contractor to explain any tricky parts of the plans, go over the work scheduled for the coming week, and outline your tasks for the week and the decisions you'll have to make. The fee for this level of service is determined on an hourly basis or as a percentage of total cost. Your architect will draw up a separate contract to cover these supervisory services.

Homeowners: *We didn't have a general contractor on our brownstone remodeling job, but we did retain the architect who designed our project. We had him visit once or twice a week to oversee the job. (To have him visit the site every day would have been pretty expensive.) We used the architect as our expert and as our heavy. That is, we told the subs we hired that their work would have to be approved by our architect before we could pay them, and we had the architect describe the jobs to the subs before they started. Knowing that he would be coming in to see that the subcontracting was done according to the building codes and the plans kept the subs on their toes.*

What a Design/Remodeling Firm Can Do for You

As you read over the descriptions of what the general contractor *and* an architect can do for you, you probably noticed that there are obvious advantages to hiring both. That is the reasoning behind the growing number of design/remodeling firms that have sprung up from coast to coast in just the last few years. As you'll recall from chapter 1, a design/remodeling firm has a designer on staff who is skilled in interviewing clients and translating their wishes into working plans. The remodeling or construction portion of the business then submits a competitive bid on those plans and, if selected, does the actual remodeling.

The advantages of using a design/remodeling firm include the following:

Better designer-contractor communication. Having the design people stay with the project all the way through construction creates a cooperative effort that is difficult to duplicate with independent professionals.

Up-to-date management and systems. Design/remodelers are experienced business-people as well as craftspeople. To earn the designation of Certified Graduate Remodeler (CGR) from the National Association of Home Builders-Remodelers Council (NAHB-RC) the contractor members must complete a series of courses on business management. The same is true of the Certified Remodeler (CR) designation awarded to members of the National Association of the Remodeling Industry (NARI) who complete a series of courses designed to improve their building skills.

Virtually all design/remodeling firms use computers to turn out the bids and contracts for their projects, track the progress of the job, and account for all the costs. Computer printouts can take some of the mystery out of the flow of funds for you the check writer.

One-stop shopping. If you use a design/remodeling firm, you only have to make one phone call to get the whole job done or to correct mistakes. Many of the subs the firm uses are permanent employees, which gives the firm much better control of their schedules and the quality of their work. When outside subs are needed, the contractor is likely to know them well.

A fixed price. The design/remodelers were among the few builders I interviewed who had no fear of submitting a fixed bid on a remodeling job. (See chapter 3 for more information on the fixed-price versus time-and-materials controversy.)

Design/Remodeler: *I just feel, short of making repairs after a fire or an earthquake, that a contractor should be able to know 99 percent of what the costs will be and offer a firm bid. I think there is too little incentive to get the job done in a timely manner when you're being paid by the hour. I also don't think it is conducive to good economic decisions. The cost-plus contractor will say, "Whatever you want, Mrs. Jones, you're the boss."*

Design/remodeling firms understand the cost of doing business and the role of profit in business survival. They're not likely to be the lowest bidder on your project, but as you'll see in the next chapter, that may not be a bad sign, particularly since it means they're apt to be in business next year.

On-time completion. With the combination of in-house subs, prebidding interviews, and a thorough understanding of the design, design/remodelers can exercise better control of a project than can a GC or an architect, which increases your chances of it coming in on schedule.

Finding Qualified Professionals

You now have a better idea of what contractors, architects, and design/remodelers can do to help you. In chapter 1, I mentioned bringing in contractors to help you as early as you can. I suggest you talk to architects and design/remodeling firms as well. This is your dance, and attendance should be by invitation only. You should screen the guests carefully, just as you would for your daughter's coming-out party, because a meaningful, long-lasting relationship is going to develop with at least one of your invitees.

Finding Contractors

There are both good and bad contractors out there. Bad can mean dishonest or just greedy or it can mean well-intentioned but unskilled or inexperienced. Your problem is to find the good ones, and the best way to do this is to conduct a systematic search. Ask your neighbors, other homeowners, people in the business, your banker, lumberyard personnel, or your local Home Builders Association or Remodelers Association for names of contractors they can recommend.

If you're in the home of friends who have had some remodeling done that you admire, ask for the name of their contractor and really question them about what it was like to work with him. If you drive by a home that is being remodeled, stop in, meet the contractor, and talk to the workers. Many contractors will put a sign out on the front lawn of the homes they are working on. The good ones will welcome you, and so will a satisfied homeowner.

If you have retained an architect, he or she will be able to recommend good contractors. After all, it is to his or her benefit to have skilled people working on the design. The folks the architect recommends may not be the least expensive, but chances are they're good builders and should be given an opportunity to bid.

It's generally not a good idea to get names out of the Yellow Pages or from ads in your local paper unless you have exhausted all other sources. Word of mouth is a far more reliable method.

Contractor: *I have been in business for twenty years, and I've never advertised except in an occasional Little League program. All my business has come through word of mouth from satisfied customers.*

Finding Architects

You can use the same methods you use to find a contractor to locate an architect as well. Another good method is to jot down architects' names while scanning magazines and newspapers for remodeling ideas. Most architects also advertise in the Yellow Pages.

As is true for every person you hire, retain, or consult with for your project, you have to find someone you can work with and whose judgment and ethics you trust. There are overinflated architects who feel their ideas are the only ones worth considering and who regard each of their projects as a monument to themselves. (Some builders swear that architecture schools must give a course on how to swell an ego.) But there are a lot of down-to-earth, practical, and creative architects able and willing to help you on your project as much or as little as you want—and at a reasonable cost.

Finding Design/Remodelers

One problem with planning to use a design/remodeling firm is that there are very few of them at this point, and you may not be able to locate one in your area. According to the National Association of Home Builders-Remodeler's Council, there are only some 278 Certified Graduate Design/Remodelers listed by the NAHB in this country. You can get a National Directory of CD/Rs by writing to: NAHB Remodeler's Council, 1201 15th Street NW, Washington, DC 20005. Or contact your local HBA or Remodelers Council for recommendations.

The National Association of the Remodeling Industry (NARI) is the other industry group. NARI has close to 6,000 members nationwide, of whom about a third have completed the Certified Remodelers (CR) qualifying course . You can get the names of firms belonging to NARI in your area by calling the national office at (703) 276-7600.

Qualifying the Professionals You Find

Finding experienced people willing to work on your project is the most important part of your job. Be sure to consider the following as you interview candidates:

Compatibility. You have to like or at least respect the professionals you choose. You will be "living" with these people for a considerable period of time under very stressful conditions. You are going to be holding long conversations, ironing out conflicts, and expressing your emotions. As one contractor suggested, "Don't hire anyone you wouldn't invite to dinner."

Honesty. If you don't trust the professionals you hire and feel you have to watch their every move and check every bill, you are in for a very unhappy time. If your contractor is out to cheat you, you probably won't even know it. There are a million places to hide overcharges and cut-rate materials where you won't find them. And leaving your wallet or loose change around as an honesty test won't work—they know about that already. The dishonest contractor will leave them alone, and the honest one will be insulted.

Judging honesty is instinctive until after you've had dealings with someone. If everyone who was dishonest looked dishonest, there wouldn't be so many successful scam operations. You have to check with the suppliers and clients your prospective contractor gives you as references. Then, rather than coming right out and asking, "Is he honest?" you might ask, "Does he offer full value on a job?" or "Is he fair?" or "Does he pay his bills and his people on time?"

Experience. Avoid the yearling professional who comes in with a low bid. You want someone who has several years' experience doing for others what you want done. I realize no one can get experience if he or she can't get a first project, but you don't want to finance that education. If you do, you're likely to have the privilege of paying for all his or her mistakes. The low bid can mean that yearling professionals want to buy their own way in by cutting profits, or it may mean they really don't know what they're doing, and you'll end up paying the price in unexpected extras or in additional time.

Architect: *I don't recommend hiring three hippies in a pickup truck looking for their first job. Nothing is cheaper, but they won't stand behind their work, and they probably don't know the best subcontractors to get.*

References. This is vital! Ask for references, then check them out *carefully.* Dig deep for real, honest opinions of the professionals you are looking to hire and the quality of their work. Good contractors, architects, and remodelers are proud of their work and will welcome your questions and expect you to talk to their clients. Given a choice, they are obviously going to give you names of their happiest customers. You might ask for their last four customers to get a better assessment. Then take the time and effort to call and visit them. Look at the work, ask lots of questions, ask for examples and stories that back up their observations, and don't be shy about talking money . . . and honesty.

Insurance and licenses. Most states require contractors, remodelers, subcontractors, and architects to be licensed with the state for their particular trade. Some states require that firms be bonded as well. Ask to see these licenses, and make sure the license numbers appear on the bids and contracts. Most states also require that contractors carry workmen's compensation insurance and liability insurance that cover both their people, the subs, and your property. If your state doesn't require it, you should.

Some contractors are able to offer lower bids by avoiding these overhead expenses. You should be aware that if a worker or sub is injured on your job and your contractor is not covered, you are next in line.

Getting down to the Final Four

If you've decided to go the route of hiring a general contractor for your job, be sure you get bids from at least three and preferably four contractors. Don't stop at one or two unless you are absolutely convinced from your investigations that you have found the perfect GC.

Even if you have gone the route of a design/remodeler, it makes sense to put the resulting plans out for bid to other contractors, because there is a human tendency to keep prices leaner when there is competition. You'll learn more about figuring out those bids in the next chapter.

CHAPTER
3

Getting Estimates
and Bids and Figuring
out What They Mean

By this point you have either a firm plan complete with working drawings or a pretty good idea of what you think you want to do. You've also narrowed the field of potential contractors down to four. Now's the time to send out invitations to bid on your project.

Estimating and bidding is an art more than a science. Keep that in mind if you demand a firm price. The problem is that every remodeling project contains surprises: a brick wall behind the plaster, a heating system that can't handle the new addition, bedrock where your septic system has to go, forty days and forty nights of rain. If you demand a firm price, your contractor will have to factor in the unknown, and his price will reflect it.

We kicked off this phase of our project by meeting with three contractors and asking them for estimates on our six alternatives. We didn't intend to use the estimates to pick the contractor; instead, we were using them to decide which remodeling plan we should use. I had told each contractor that I didn't expect him to live with his estimate because it was based on so little actual information and because I was asking him to come up with it while sitting at our table. What happened is what I suspect happens in a lot of bidding situations. Each contractor gave me a rough figure he thought I wanted to hear, a figure also intended to keep him in the running against the competition. That these figures bore little resemblance to the eventual cost of the proposed task was, I now know, to be expected.

The estimates we got, which ranged from $40,000 to $50,000, turned out to be about half

Bidding Terms to Know

The **estimate** is the amount a contractor thinks the job will cost before he does his serious calculations and while he is trying to get the job. It is not a figure to be taken very seriously.

The **bid** is the amount of money a contractor thinks your job will actually cost, plus his overhead and whatever profit he requires. The bid usually includes a general list of materials and labor. Since bids are what many people use to make their final selection, a contractor will make every effort to keep his bid low. Of course, a low bid does not necessarily lead to the lowest-cost job, as you will see later.

The **contract** or **agreement** is legally binding and should provide an itemized list of the materials and supplies for the job. It should also stipulate what you and your contractor agree is the scope of the project, how it will be done, and the accounting procedures to be used. It should provide a schedule and method of payment. Any items not specifically included become extras, as will any changes you authorize; both will be added to the final cost.

what we eventually paid. In the end we went with the contractor who suggested adding a second floor. So, in effect, we selected our contractor based on his design ideas rather than on his estimate. We also checked out his references, found out he had a reputation for honesty and good work, and saw examples of his work. (In fact, he himself took us to look at other jobs he had done.) It didn't hurt that we also liked him.

What we did, I have since learned, was short-circuit the bidding process I am about to describe by preselecting our contractor. The advantage of this approach is that your contractor can help you, as ours did, with the planning process. The disadvantage is you don't get to see any competitive bids.

Once we selected our contractor, he worked with us to come up with the final design and created the working drawings, including the various elevations of the house, that we needed to get our plan accepted by our local Historical District Commission. He then prepared an agreement or contract that outlined what he would build, what materials and supplies he would use, and how much it would cost. Suddenly our project had advanced to the $80,000 level. With this figure in hand we were able to go to banks to refinance our mortgage.

Was this figure accurate? Did it represent our total and final cost for the project? No. And yet it was arrived at by a contractor knowledgeable in the costs and prices involved in construction who already had the job and was simply trying to determine how much money we needed. Since this money was eventually going to be used to pay him, it would make sense on his part to be sure it was accurate. If his "bid" was inaccurate, and it was, think of the problems encountered by the contractor who is bidding against competition.

How Do Contractors Bid a Remodeling Job?

Many magazine articles on construction and remodeling tell the homeowner to get a firm contract with a firm price from contractors. The only problem with this advice is that many contractors have learned it only makes sense to bid remodeling jobs on what they call a *time-and-materials* or *cost-plus* basis. Because they don't want to guarantee what the job will cost, they offer to keep track of the costs, add in their profit, and send you the bill.

Their reluctance to name a precise figure is understandable. In all but the most rudimentary remodeling projects, coming up with an exact bid is like estimating the time it will take to drive from Boston to New York City without knowing the weather, the route to be taken, and the driver, and without allowing for any emergencies or detours. If the low estimate will win the contract, the savvy bidder will assume perfect weather, no traffic tie-ups, and no detours and will allow no time to get gas and food.

How would that look in writing? The bid would state, "Estimate based on perfect weather, 50 miles per gallon, all thruway travel, and no stoplights." Can that be done? Of course not.

Let's translate that example to bidding on a theoretical bathroom remodeling job in an older home. You've invited two contractors in to look at your ideas for redoing your bathroom and to submit bids. You might even have made up a list of the items you want: new tub, new shower, new linoleum, new toilet, new sink, and new plumbing fixtures.

Contractor #1 submits a bid covering his labor for removal of the old tub, sink, toilet, plumbing fixtures and flooring and installing the new items:

Labor: forty hours at $40 per hour or $1,600. Allowance for purchase of the new items as listed: $1,000. The actual items TBS (to be selected) by the owner at a later date. Any additional labor or materials needed but not listed in the bid or contract will be charged extra on a time and materials basis.

Total bid: $2,600

Contractor #2 is an experienced builder who knows that houses that are more than forty years old are ripe for plumbing problems. Her bid includes removal of the old tub, sink, toilet, and plumbing fixtures plus replacement of pipes from the basement to the bathroom. She also noticed signs of water damage around the tub and includes replacement of the underlayment as well as the new linoleum on the floor. When she asked you about the tile around the tub, you pointed out that you assumed it went without saying that the new tub would also mean new tile work. Her bid includes replacing the backing as well as the cost of purchasing and installing the tile. It also includes the estimated cost of changing the electrical outlets and patching the wall in order to move the sink a couple of feet to one side, as you requested. Her bid looks like this:

Labor to remove and replace old bathroom fixtures, replace piping, remove and replace subflooring, lay new linoleum, remove and replace tile around tub, and move electrical outlets: eighty hours at $40 per hour or $3,200. Basic materials needed: lumber, flooring, tile, Sheetrock, mastic, nails, etc. at $1,600. Allowance for new fixtures to be selected by homeowner: $2,500. Any additional labor and materials needed but not listed in bid will be charged extra on a time-and-materials basis.

Total bid: $7,300.

Which bid would you take? Probably even the stingiest homeowner would take the higher bid as the more accurate assessment of the work.

In the actual bidding process, the reasoning behind the bids you get is often not as clear as in this example. Some contractors cut down on their overhead by not being bonded or properly licensed and not carrying insurance and workmen's comp. It allows them to bid lower, but if there is an accident on your site, you become liable.

Some contractors consider their bid a fixed price for doing the job and will charge no more even if they lose money. They will anticipate problems and allow for them. Their bids will tend to be high. Other contractors regard their initial bid as a starting point in the billing process. Their bids will enumerate the things they will do, but there will be no provision for surprises or the simplest changes. The cost of those will be tacked on. That's why you can't just look at the bottom line of the bids. You have to try to determine what each includes.

Contractor: *You have to remember there are two kinds of contractors bidding out there. There is the guy who will bid everything in the job and give you a complete price of, say, $50,000. Then there is the guy who appears to have bid less with a bid of $38,000. Most homeowners would go with the lower bid. But that low bidder knows where there are apt to be problems he hasn't allowed for in his bid, such as the old piping behind the bathroom wall that will have to be replaced and the rotted sills under the windows. These come under the heading of extras that will be needed and charged for. By the end of the job, his costs wind up at $75,000, and the homeowner wonders what hit him.*

Every contractor and builder has had to go through a learning process. The honest ones will admit they are just as confused about how to bid as the homeowners are about how to evaluate the bids.

Contractor: *When I started to build, I frequently got screwed because I didn't know how to bid. I would bid the basic job as it appeared on the plans without making allowances for those hidden problems that always come up. I would get the bid and lose money on the job. When I wised up and began to increase my bids to allow for those problems, I lost out on the jobs because I was too high. Some guys, I learned, would lowball their bids and then hit the owners hard with extras: "You wanted a roof? The plans don't mention a roof. That will be extra." I now combine a basic bid with a separate list of areas where I think problems might come up and the possible additional costs.*

There is a saying in construction that the guy who gets the job is the one who was the most wrong.

Builder: *My partner and I used to be in the roofing business together, and we would bid jobs and lose them to someone who bid way below us. We would talk to the winners and ask how they came up with such a low bid, and frequently they would say they just drove by the job and made a guess. How can you compete with that? And six months later the owner would call us to come in and finish the job because the low bidder had taken the roof off the house and couldn't afford to put it back on.*

Of course, the magazines that promote firm bids are doing so to protect you from the hazard of add-on costs. But that puts the contractor in a bind.

Home Builder: *If homeowners want a fixed price, they are, in effect, treating us like an insurance company. They want us to assume all the risks of their project so they will know the exact cost. We then have to assume the worst and estimate accordingly. The homeowner in this age of consumerism has to grow up. The contractor is not his mentor, he's a guy out there trying to earn a living. If the homeowner wants the lowest cost, he has to start accepting some of the risk. He owns that wall and he also owns all the problems behind it.*

One builder, when I quoted a homeowner who bragged about her builder coming in right on bid, responded, "I can come in right on bid too... Just let me bid high enough."

Builder: *A firm bid from a contractor will cost a lot. Because even with a contracted bid, as the building is exposed, the homeowner invariably changes his mind. For example, a homeowner will ask you how much it will cost to take out a wall? Oh, a couple of hundred dollars. You do it, then he says, "Gee, I really would like doors there," and his $200 bid is shot. I make more money on a firm bid than I do on cost-plus.*

Some builders have handled the problem of coming up with accurate yet competitive bids by simply refusing to get involved in what they regard as a completely artificial process.

Builder: *How do I bid on remodeling? I don't. I only take on remodeling jobs on a cost-plus basis—It's the only way that's fair to me and fair to the client. My advice to homeowners is not to base your decision to buy the services of a contractor entirely on price. Base your decision on the experience of the contractor and on recommendations from his former clients.*

Three Basic Approaches to Bidding

1. Time and materials (or **cost-plus**). The contractor estimates the amount of materials that will be required for the job and the number of hours it will take to complete and adds 10 to 15 percent for his profit. He comes up with a rough estimate that you can take to the bank for your loan.

> *Advantages:* The final costs will be based on the actual time spent and materials used on the job itself. If surprise complications arise, they will add to the cost, but if they have been anticipated in the estimate and do not happen, the cost will come down. With an honest contractor the homeowner will pay only for the work that is done.

> *Disadvantages:* A high level of trust is required for this approach. A dishonest or even just a slightly greedy contractor can cost the homeowner dearly. An architect or the homeowner should be available to monitor the amount of time actually taken to do the job. This is where the inexperienced worker will cost the most, because he will make mistakes and take longer to figure jobs out. You pay as much per hour for slow work as you do for fast work.

2. Cost per square foot. This method works best in new construction such as an addition, where the variables are more under the builder's control. Even then it differs with the rooms being worked on. The kitchen and bathroom are the most expensive per square foot because of the costly items that go into them and the relatively small size of the rooms.

> *Advantages:* You can get a quick estimate based on the square footage on the first go-round.

> *Disadvantages:* A price per square foot is virtually useless as a basis for a contract. It is just too vague.

3. Firm price. The contractor, working from his plans or your architect's, lists the type and amount of materials he will need, the hours of labor he anticipates for the project, the costs of the subcontracted jobs (which he, in turn, sends out for bid by the subs), and the cost or allowances he has made for appliances, cabinets, fixtures, etc. His profit or percentage markup is also included. The contract will stipulate the method and time of payment.

Advantages: If the contractor runs into delays or surprises in jobs that are included in the contract, the price stays the same for the homeowner. This sounds like an air-tight agreement that limits your expenditures and ensures your getting exactly what you expect at a fixed cost, right? Well, maybe.

Disadvantages: If a contractor is forced to come up with a firm price that he is going to have to live with, he must include a large "fudge factor" to cover the unknown and the unexpected. And if you change your mind or want to add something to the job after it starts, that becomes an "extra." The final cost can be considerably more than the original contract bid.

Coping with Surprises

The unexpected is the rule rather than the exception in remodeling. For that reason a contractor should conduct a thorough investigation of your project before he or she bids. That means the contractor should check out your heating system if you plan to add space, evaluate your electrical service if you plan to add new appliances to your kitchen, and know the age of your house and the capacity of your present septic system if you are planning to update the plumbing or add a bathroom.

Builder: *There's nothing like taking the time to really look a job over before you shoot off your mouth. I had a job that started with, "Will you knock out this wall between my two small upstairs bedrooms and make one big one?" I said, "Sure, it will cost about $1,000." Well, I got into it and found that this wall had all the wiring for the downstairs running through the middle of it, which I didn't know about because I hadn't crawled up into the attic to look. When we took the wall down, I finally got up into the attic. I discovered that previous owners had removed a chimney and, rather than carrying the bricks downstairs, had spread them all over the attic. So there was a ton of bricks up there slowly pushing the ceiling down. The same previous owner knew that the ceiling was coming down, so he had put in a drop ceiling to cover it.*

In the end, this "easy" job ended up costing $4,000.

When it comes to the difficult task of seeing through walls, one contractor suggested an additional step that could eliminate at least some unknowns:

Contractor: *Let's say it's an old house, and the homeowner wants to tear out a wall between two rooms. I'd give him a bid, but I'd also ask him to pay me for two or three hours of my time to tear open the wall and see what is behind it. I'd say to him, "If you want four guys to bid this contract, fine: This weekend, tear open that wall yourself and show your prospective contractors what's behind it, so they know what they're bidding on." Most people will not tear open their wall because they are not really sure whether they will go ahead with the project, even though it would only take about fifty dollars worth of Sheetrock and taping to repair the hole if they decided not to go ahead. Yet they ask the contractors to risk thousands of dollars bidding on the unknown.*

Not all your surprises will be hidden behind the walls. A devious contractor can spring quite a few on the unsuspecting homeowner.

Builder: *Watch out for the contractor who tells you not to worry about what kind of bathroom tile or cabinets you are getting. When you ask for a firm price, he'll tell you he is handling it with allowances (an amount he writes in to cover the cost) for each of these items. But what he's doing is trying to get the job by schmoozing you past all the critical and costly decisions. He knows there is a big price difference between wallpaper at eighteen dollars a roll and two coats of good paint, between Formica countertops and slate, between plated bathroom fixtures and brass. What he may be doing is calculating all low-end materials for his bid while leaving you the option to select, at additional cost, the fixtures and materials you really want. This is especially true if you have told him what the other contractors have bid and he knows what price he has to beat.*

Comparing Bids: Apples to Apples or Kumquats to Cherries?

Asked what he thought about as he sat in the nose cone of the space shuttle just before launch, one of the early astronauts said that he reflected on the complexity of the machinery and the fact that each and every part had been built by the lowest bidder. Governmental agencies are required by law to go with the low bidder, but you can use some discretion.

There are literally hundreds of steps in any remodeling process, and you should have some knowledge of the trades if you are going to make a true apples-to-apples comparison of the bids you receive. Begin by doing some research at your local lumberyard and in the showrooms. Price the cost of plywood and two-by-fours and price the plumbing and electrical fixtures *you* want. Your builder may be able to get a better price, but at least you won't be surprised by a higher cost.

Another approach is to keep the bidding on the basic proposal separate from any allowances for contingencies or surprises. Then have the contractors list the areas where they think problems might be encountered and cost those out separately. This helps level the playing field for the contractor who is trying to give you an honest, realistic bid by anticipating problem areas.

Negotiating with the Bidders

There is no problem with your sharing a contractor's bid with other contractors as long as you also make clear what each intends to do and the quality of the materials each will furnish for his price. The contractors will understand this approach. Don't play the game like a poker hand. Blind bidding, where no one knows what the other has bid, is counterproductive. Let the bidders know what they are up against. If a good GC sees another bid that is totally out of line with reality, he will warn you. He may even go back to his own drawing board, sharpen his pencil, and give you a better bid.

Builder: *On a recent job I figured my cost-plus profit was $40,000 for an addition to a home in an upscale town. Then I looked at the job, I looked at the neighborhood, I looked at the people, and figured no way would this job go out this cheap; so I pushed my bid to $55,000. The owner called and told me I was in the high middle of four bids. He said he liked the way I talked and my feeling for old houses and suggested that if we could reach a price, I would be his man.*

I asked him what he wanted to pay, and he said his budget was around $50,000. I already had a good profit in my bid, but I knew there was a chance of some problems with the foundation. I added a line to the bid saying that if we hit ledge or encountered ground problems we would split the cost difference. I dropped my bid from $55,000 to $51,850 and got the job at a price that was right for both of us.

When it comes time for you to go out for bids, invite four contractors to submit bids. Then throw out the high and low bids and negotiate with the two in the middle, which should be fairly close together and probably close to the price you should be paying.

How Homeowners Handle the Bidding Process

I tried to find homeowners who were proud of the way they had handled their negotiations with their contractor. I succeeded in locating only two. One got multiple bids, and the other worked closely with a single contractor to obtain a good price that was fair to both parties. All the other homeowners said they would do it differently if they were to do it again.

The most successful negotiator I interviewed owned an inn and was already on her fourth remodeling project in as many homes. She was still learning, but she had worked out a bidding system that saved her time and money.

Inn Owner: *When I start a remodeling project, I always start with a budget I can afford, and I always stay within my budget. I've never gone over, and that's doing two kitchens and three bathrooms.*

How do I price? I start with the big things. If I'm doing a kitchen, I go out and price the cabinets I want. Then I get at least three estimates to do the work, and I'm careful of the bids that are too high or too low.

I also got firm contracts on the bathrooms. The contractors made the same money whether it took them two weeks or ten weeks. They could have been at this forever; as it was they were neophytes at the contracting business and took eight weeks on two baths when they thought it would take three. I would never sign a contract if it were not a firm price.

Another homeowner couple felt they got a satisfactory contract and minimized the risk inherent in a time-and-materials bid by doing some homework at the local lumberyard and by being straightforward with the one contractor they invited to bid.

Homeowners: *For the materials costs, the contractor gave us an estimate down to the nails, then he estimated the number of hours it would take and multiplied this by his per-hour cost. And that was his bid. We told him that if he ran into problems on some part of his bid, we would not hold his feet to the fire, so to speak. We did that so he wouldn't feel obligated to put in some kind of allowance for problems and pad the bill to cover them. We agreed that any extras would be at the rate per hour he had given and that we would meet with him whenever a decision was needed to move up or down in the quality of a material. If an upgrade was called for, such as having ¾-inch plywood underlayment instead of ½-inch, he would give us a figure for the additional cost and let us make the decision. We usually went for the upgrades except for using galvanized roofing nails in the slate roof instead of the traditional copper. As a result we have already lost a few slates on our "lifetime" slate roof. Unfortunately, we cut quality where it really mattered!*

Most homeowners felt they should have done more homework.

> **Homeowners:** *We took the first estimate from the first general contractor who came to the house. It was for $70,000. Three months after we had accepted the bid he had not started the job, so we dropped him. The next GC came in at $45,000 for the same job. Then we added a basement and other stuff as we went along, and the final bill went to $70,000. Was it the right amount? We still don't know. Who do you trust? What did we really need? Could the old heating system have served the addition? Did we really need a new septic system? All those "ifs" could make a $20,000 difference.*

These homeowners, both professional people, tried to hurry up the selection process. They hired an architect to design their addition who was so meticulous that he built a model to show how the addition would blend into the original 1800s saltbox, but the homeowners did not use him to help evaluate the bids or to oversee the project. Many of the "ifs" they mentioned could have been ironed out if they had worked more closely with the architect or had invited a few more contractors in to bid on the project and asked them questions. Unfortunately, they deluded themselves into thinking that remodeling is a simple, straightforward process.

If you still can't make heads or tails of the bids you receive, consider hiring another contractor or an architect to act as a consultant. When one homeowner got four bids ranging from $45,000 to $96,000 he hired a contractor-friend to sit down and create a set of specifications to use to compare bids.

What the contractor found when he compared each bid was that each contractor had bid on what *he* wanted to do. No one really paid strict attention to the specs called for in the plans. The low bidder did not have 10 inches of insulation in the attic, had two instead of three coats of a less expensive urethane on the wood floors, and allowed for only bottom-of-the-line fixtures and cabinets. The high bidder had included everything the homeowners asked for but was basically overpriced. The homeowner's contractor-friend helped him decide on the contractor who bid $84,000. His bid at least showed he had made an honest effort to come to grips with reality.

Of course, reality sometimes plays no part at all in the bidding process. But usually it's the homeowner, not the contractor, who's unrealistic.

> **Builder:** *A friend of mine asked me about a deck she wanted to get done and mentioned that she had one bid for $8,000 she thought might be too high. Well, I thought, that's a big enough job that it might pay for me to take a look at it. No way was that an $8,000 job. I costed it out and offered to do it for $4,000 as soon as I got back from a week's vacation. When I got back she said she had already given it out to someone else. Another guy had come in and he said he would do it for $400.*
>
> *"Fine," I said. "Don't call me when it falls down." The bidding went from $8,000 to $400, and she had no idea in the world what the job was worth. I'll bet the guy who did it took it to four grand by the time he was done.*

The Bottom Line on Getting Bids

Say you're gearing up for a fairly extensive remodeling project, like enlarging and rebuilding your kitchen. Based on my own experience and on all my interviews with homeowners and builders, here is how I recommend you approach the process of getting bids and making the final selection of a contractor.

Start by knowing exactly what the project involves and what you want done. That's not easy, so be sure to take extra time to plan. If necessary, retain an architect on an hourly basis to help you solve problems in the planning stage.

Consider having an architect create a set of working drawings as well. Then bring your floor plan to a lumberyard and ask them do a *take-off*—in other words, to list the quantity, quality, and price of all the materials needed. Also ask them to create a *schedule* of the various windows and doors called for along with their prices. Then go to electrical- and plumbing-supply houses for your electrical and plumbing schedules. Research prices yourself for as many appliances and fixtures as practical.

In this way you will, in effect, prepare your own bid. You'll go through the same steps a contractor will to make his bid except for adding overhead and profit. With these lists and prices in hand, you have a fighting chance of evaluating and comparing the bids of the contractors you audition for the job.

The next step is to find good contractors by using the methods discussed earlier. Invite up to six contractors to see the job and to meet you. Ask each for references and a list of her last four jobs. Check out those references and visit her clients' homes to see the work and talk to the people involved. Get their real feelings rather than settling for a polite "she's okay" over the phone.

Now you're ready to solicit bids from four of the contractors. Give each a set of working drawings, specifications, and your list of appliances and fixtures. If your house is more than forty years old, consider opening up a wall to let the contractors see what they're getting into.

If you are using an architect, he or she can help you sort out the bids. If the bids vary widely, throw out the highest and lowest unless the bidders can justify them. Then openly discuss the bids with the two contractors in the middle in an effort to understand them better and perhaps get a better price.

Finally, select the contractor you get along with, whose work is good, and whose references you trust. Then work out a good, strong, fair contract.

You'll find a sample proposal or bid on the following pages, furnished by a design/remodeler. In its present form it is called a *proposal*, but as soon as it is signed by both parties, it becomes an *agreement*.

CHAPTER
4

Contracts
and How to Read Them

The days of plans drawn on the backs of envelopes, a handshake, and a promise to "work out the money part later" are gone, if they ever existed. Now, many states require a properly executed remodeling contract, or the contractor runs the risk of not being able to collect any payments.

What Is a Contract?

In the simplest terms a contract is really just an agreement between you and your contractor (or architect) in which you describe what you want done and your contractor describes what he will do, who and what he will use to do it, how much it will cost, and the terms of payment—a comparatively straightforward, simple statement of understanding between two people. But, as one builder observed, "It starts out as an agreement and it only becomes a contract when something goes wrong and the lawyers get hold of it."

Who Should Write the Contract?

The answer to this question isn't necessarily "the contractor." After all, the one who writes the contract gets to put in what he or she wants to put in and leave out what he or she wants. This is an advantage.

Some states mandate the inclusion of certain things in a remodeling contract. But usually the requirements are so basic that homeowners still have to look out for their own interests.

Instead of simply accepting your contractor's standard contract, you might try your hand at writing your own contract. There is plenty of help available from forms supplied by the AIA (see below).

What Parts Should a Contract Contain?

From my talks with contractors and from a review of a proposal for a standard remodeling contract still being considered, I would recommend that a remodeling contract contain the following:

An agreement page in which the contractor, architect, or homeowner outlines the work to be done in sufficient detail that the scope of the project and builder responsibilities are clear. It should include a procedure for making changes. One good way to judge the competence of a contractor is by how complete, accurate, and timely his Change Order Forms are. Well-documented change orders are a sign of a GC who is in control, organized, and knows what is going on.

Design/Builder: *The original contracts or agreements are usually pretty clear, but as a job progresses and changes come up, the paperwork tends to get a little sloppy. It is change orders and additional work that create most of the friction in any remodeling project.*

The agreement page, or pages, if needed, should end with a clear statement of those things that are *not included.*

A specification page in which the quality level or brand names and model numbers of all the materials and products called for in the agreement are listed. If they have not yet been selected, this page should clearly state that the items are still to be selected (TBS) by the homeowner.

The GC should prepare a list of the choices you must make, from window styles to kitchen cabinets to light fixtures. If you accepted a firm bid from your contractor (as opposed to working on a time-and-materials basis), he should tell you how much he allocated for each item. Keep those allocated amounts in mind so you don't go crazy in the bath-fixture showroom or in any of the fifty other places where you'll have an irresistible opportunity to inflate the final cost of your project.

The point at which you choose your fixtures and so forth is the point at which you will begin to realize how good or bad your contractor's original bid was. Two thousand dollars may seem like a lot of money for kitchen cabinets until you walk into the showroom and discover that it buys you bottom-of-the-line cabinets with none of the special features you wanted. Maybe the contractor who estimated $8,000 for your kitchen cabinets knew what he was talking about after all.

I hope he is still on your list of possible winners.

A drawing page or attachment with the final working drawings for the project. Hide all the preliminary sketches and any other rejected floor plans, and make any future alterations on this "official" set of plans.

Addendum and conditions pages. These will include any specific conditions expressed by the contractor plus applicable standard addendum forms from the list available from the AIA. (See the section on AIA contract forms at the end of this chapter.) These will define the terms used in the agreement and will also furnish provisions for settling disputes.

A Look At an Actual Contract

If you're not up to supplying your own contract (and most homeowners aren't), you'll probably end up signing a contract supplied by your contractor. These vary, of course, but the proposal reproduced on the following pages—an actual proposal by a reputable design/remodeling firm—is a good example of the form and wording you can expect to see for a fixed-price project.

Sample Kitchen Remodeling Proposal: an Item-by-item Review

Let's go through the sample proposal line by line and see what each item could mean to the homeowner.

(A) Name, address, etc.

This section is pretty straightforward, but it does contain some of the basic essentials such as the name, address, and telephone number of the company you're dealing with. If you don't see your contractor's license number here, make sure it appears elsewhere in the contract. (This particular contractor has put it under the start date on page 2.)

SAMPLE KITCHEN REMODELING PROPOSAL
Building Company Name
Address/Telephone Number

A

PROPOSAL SUBMITTED TO:_____ PHONE: _____ DATE:_____

STREET: _____ JOB NAME: _____

CITY, STATE, ZIP: _____ JOB LOCATION: _____

ARCHITECT: _Builder's design_ DATE OF PLANS: _____ JOB PHONE: _____

B

   We Propose hereby to furnish material and labor—complete in accordance with specifications below, for the sum:
   (Written Total) Sixteen thousand nine hundred and five   Dollars ($16,905).

C

Payment to be made as follows:
 15% down payment, 25% when work commences, 25% when roughs are completed,
 25% when fixtures are set, balance upon substantial completion.

D

   All material is guaranteed to be as specified. All work to be completed in a workmanlike manner according to standard practices. Any alteration or deviation from specifications below involving extra costs will be executed only upon written orders and will become an extra charge over and above the estimate. All agreements contingent upon strikes, accidents, or delays beyond our control. Owner to carry fire, tornado, and other necessary insurance. Our workers are fully covered by workmen's compensation Insurance.

Signature of builder.

_____

E

Note: This proposal may be withdrawn by us if not accepted within _____5____ days.

We hereby submit specifications and estimates for:

"Kitchen Remodeling"

F

TO INCLUDE:
Plans/Permit—Permit not included. Simple kitchen layout plans included.
Demolition/Cleanups—provide plastic at door openings and drop-cloth runners on finish floors. Cleanups as work progresses. Remove existing underlayment and finish floor.
Cabinets/Counters/Removals—remove and discard existing cabinets, counters as directed by owner. Existing refrigerator moved to another adjacent room for temporary use during project. Old appliances discarded by homeowner unless specified otherwise.
Structural—relocate walls at pantry for new layout. Create new stub wall with Sheetrock cornerbead edges. Walls and floor patched and repaired.
Underlayment—builder to install APA plywood underlayment per manufacturer's specs with screws and ring nails.
Walls/Ceiling—½" Sheetrock applied to new walls and repaired ceiling area. Taped/spackled three coats and sanded smooth. Ceiling to be sprayed with medium-density spray after scraping and using stain-kill paint sealer. Wallpaper removal, if required, is not included.

F

Plumbing—disconnect existing equipment (assumes all valves are operational and waste and supply lines are adequate). Connect new fixtures and appliances (appliances by owner). Sink and faucet allowance to be $200.00. ISE garbage disposer included. Ice maker hookup included.

Electrical—disconnect existing appliances and fixtures. Relocate table hanging light. Add new recess light (supplied by builder) in sink soffit. Existing plugs updated with GFI plugs as per code. Add four recess lights (Brand and model numbers) off existing switch (change to dimmer) in kitchen.

Heating—none included.

Cooking Ventilation—no duct work included. Recirculating hood fan planned.

Flooring—new sheet goods vinyl flooring (to be selected—TBS) installed after installation of new underlayment. Figure $18/s.y. retail cost plus tax for flooring allowance. Provide and install vinyl cove base under cabinet toe spaces and behind the refrigerator. Metal edges may be necessary at junction of other floor materials.

Cabinets—Cabinets to be chosen. Kraftmaid pickled maple cabinets budgeted. ($4,000 allowed). Installation cost included.

Counters—built up edge plastic laminate counters with 4" splash included. Owner to wallpaper above the splash.

General Carpentry—baseboard replaced and install new materials similar to existing. Other trim to remain unless specified otherwise. Assumes that window and door trims are not cut or notched from previous kitchen layout and thus can be reused as is.

G

NOT INCLUDED:

Appliances—supplied/delivered by others/owner. Set by builder.

Paint/decorate—by owner.

Electrical Fixtures—by owner unless specified otherwise.

H

TOTAL BUDGET = $16,905.00

I

Approx start date = xx/xx/xx
Approx completing date = xx/xx/xx

J

Connecticut Home Improvement Registration # 000000

K

Contract Addendum has been read by customer and is part of this agreement.

L

TERMS: All unpaid balances after 30 days will run at 1½% per month on the unpaid balance, 18% per annum. All costs of collection including a reasonable attorney's fee will be charged to customer in the event this matter is placed for collection. You have three days to cancel this contract.

M

Acceptance of Proposal - The above prices, specifications, and conditions are satisfactory and are hereby accepted. You are authorized to do the work as specified. Payment will be made as outlined above.

N

Date of Acceptance:_____

Signature _____

Signature _____

(B) We propose

A very brief description of what the remodeler agrees to provide: materials and labor. Also the quoted price, which, as we shall see, is not what the job is going to cost.

(C) Payment schedule

You'll notice that this contract calls for 15 percent of the total at the time of signing and an additional 25 percent when work commences. This comes to 40 percent of the total as a down payment.

This amount of "up front" money is not uncommon in a kitchen or bathroom remodeling job because so much of the job involves the purchase of expensive cabinets and fixtures. Other payments are due when "rough carpentry" is complete (25 percent) and when the fixtures are "set" (25 percent).

Unless you are putting on an addition, remodeling of existing space does not usually involve heavy materials costs. Thus, the payments will be more evenly spread throughout the job.

(D) Standard fine-print paragraph

This statement offers the homeowner some standard guarantees for the quality of the work done and materials used. Ideally, terms such as *workmanlike manner* and *standard practices* ought to be defined in the attached addendum, but even if they're not, you can be sure that they mean something to an arbitrator or judge.

Notice the statement "Any alteration or deviation from the specifications below involving extra cost . . . will become extra costs over and above the estimate." Here the contractor is protecting himself from surprises and changes requested by the owner. He is also taking the businesslike approach of stating that all such changes must be in writing. He further protects himself by saying he is not responsible for on-time completion as stipulated by the specific date in the contract or additional costs due to circumstances beyond his control.

The insurance question is handled by having the homeowners insure their home and the contractor cover his own workers.

(E) Time limit on bid

The remodeler has set a five-day time limit for the homeowners' acceptance of the bid. It is not uncommon for clients to sit on proposals for weeks, months, or even years and then expect the amount quoted to be the same.

(F) To include:

Plans/Permit—The fact that the permit is not included means the homeowners must apply for their own permit. This bothers me because the issuing agency will hold the person requesting the permit responsible for conforming to the local regulations. In fact, the builder should apply for the permit, and the clause should be revised to read, *"Builder will apply for all permits. Owner will be billed for any fees involved."*

Demolition/Cleanups—Many contracts don't cover this subject. I would like to see the phrase *broom clean at end of each day*. It should also specify who is responsible for getting rid of the trash, as disposal of building refuse can be an expensive and time-consuming part of any remodeling project.

Cabinets/Counters/Removals—Notice that this clause makes provisions for the homeowners to have the use of the refrigerator—albeit in the living room—for the duration of the project. It also requires them to dispose of the old appliances, a point they may want to negotiate.

Walls/Ceiling—The remodeler offers a clear picture of what will be done to the walls and ceiling, but he is also protecting himself against the unknown. If the owners decide the wallpaper must be removed, it will be at extra cost. This could mean one of two things: either removing the wallpaper is a remote possibility or the contractor has left out the cost in order to offer a lower bid.

Plumbing—The contractor further protects himself by clearly stating his assumption that "all valves are operational and waste and supply lines are adequate." If they are not "operational and adequate," their replacement would mean considerable additional cost to the homeowner. Like the wallpaper above, the need may be remote or it could be a hidden cost.

A $200 allowance for the sink and faucet may well be too little. To avoid unpleasant surprises, homeowners are wise to select and price their fixtures ahead of time so they'll know the actual cost.

Electrical—Everything seems to be covered. When you find terms like *GFI*, ask for a definition. Don't try to pretend you know.

Heating—Since the space is staying the same, the existing heating should be sufficient.

Cooking Ventilation—New duct work is not needed with the type of hood fan called for.

Flooring—The homeowners would be wise to price the flooring they want in order to determine if the allowance is adequate. Metal edges may be necessary, but we don't know whether they are covered by the agreement or not.

Cabinets—The cabinets have yet to be selected (TBS) by the owners, but the builder has based his allowance of $4,000 on a particular brand and model of cabinets. If the owners select an upscale brand or style, the cost could easily double. Better to price the cabinets you want in advance.

Notice that installation is included, as it should be.

Counters—The owners have agreed to purchase and put up the wallpaper, probably to save money. We did this in our kitchen three years after we moved in. It was a manageable one-evening task.

General Carpentry—Notice the contractor's assumptions that the window and door trim will be usable. If the trim has been notched or cut, the homeowners' cost will rise.

(G) Not included:

This is an excellent heading to include in a contract. It helps to avoid misunderstandings and incorrect assumptions.

Appliances—The proposal doesn't include the cost of appliances. If a stove, refrigerator, microwave oven, and dishwasher are called for, the owners can expect to need considerably more funds than the total quoted in the proposal.

Paint/Decorate—The purchase of paint or wallpaper is the responsibility of the owners, who presumably will do their own work to save some money.

Electrical Fixtures—It would seem that most of the electrical fixtures are covered in the proposal, but any additional fixtures would be an additional cost.

(H) Total budget

Here we have the cost of what the builder has agreed to perform and provide. You can be sure this is not what the project is going to cost. We know the owners are going to have to purchase all the appliances, some light fixtures, and wallpaper and possibly pay a building permit fee and a fee for hauling away debris and old appliances. They then have to hope the existing plumbing and the trim around the window and door are reusable or they will have to pay to replace them. After they add in all these possibilities they will know the total cost only if they can live with the allowances for cabinets and flooring.

(I) Approximate starting and completing dates

Since this project is being done by a design/remodeler who has his own subs, these dates may be accurate if there are no surprises. Some owners have suggested levying a penalty fee for every day the contractor is late. I don't think it is a good idea. It starts the relationship off on an adversarial basis, and, to be fair, would you be willing to pay him an incentive fee for every day he cuts off the construction time?

(J) State home improvement registration number

A good thing to see on any proposal or contract.

(K) Contract addendum

This states that the homeowner has read the attached pages (not reproduced), which contain definitions of terminology used in the proposal and the general conditions of the contract (see AIA forms, below). The material contained in the addendum will probably only come into use if there is an argument between the owner and the builder. It is written in legal but understandable English and should be read before signing the proposal.

(L) Terms

Describes what will happen if the homeowners don't pay on time. It also alerts the owners that they have three days to change their minds after they have signed the proposal.

(M) Acceptance of proposal

With their signatures the homeowners accept the offer, change this "proposal" to a "contract," and authorize the builder to start work (after three days).

(N) Date and two signatures

If a married couple is hiring the contractor, both the husband and wife must sign. The date of acceptance starts the time clock running on the homeowners' right to cancel.

American Institute of Architects (AIA) Contract Forms

If you retain an architect, he or she will undoubtedly prepare an agreement for services based on one of many contract forms available from the AIA. The architect will then prepare another contract between you and your building contractor from another AIA form. These standard AIA agreement forms have been developed over more than seventy-five years of experience and have been tested repeatedly in the courts throughout the United States. Fortunately, the AIA makes their forms available to the public at prices ranging from 45 cents to $4.20.

The forms are tailored to specific situations (the number in parentheses is the order number):

- Owner-Contractor Agreement Form—Stipulated Sum (A101)
- Abbreviated Owner-Contractor Agreement Form for Small Construction Contracts— Stipulated Sum (A107)
- Owner-Contractor Agreement Form—Cost Plus Fee (A111)
- Standard Form of Agreement Between Owner and Design/Builder (A191)
- Standard Form of Agreement Between Owner and Architect (B141)
- Standard Form of Agreement Between Owner and Architect—Construction Management Edition (B141/CM)
- Standard Form of Agreement Between Owner and Architect for Designated Services (B161)
- General Conditions of the Contract for Construction (A201)

How to Order AIA Forms

The above list includes only a fraction of the forms available. You can get a complete listing of forms and their prices though your local or state AIA. You can obtain their telephone number by asking virtually any architect or by calling the national headquarters at (202) 626-7300.

The forms can be ordered over the phone and charged to your MasterCard or Visa with a minimum purchase of $15.00. Order enough forms to let you compare the various options open to you, and fill out the ones you like best. Also, some forms are designed to be used in conjunction with other forms, such as the General Conditions of the Contract for Construction. Your AIA representative will explain when you call.

How to Use AIA Forms

The forms are of the fill-in-the-blanks variety and are intended to be used as a consumable—that is, the original document purchased by the user is intended to be consumed in the course of being used. Once filled in, you may reproduce up to ten copies for distribution to the parties involved.

Each form comes with detailed and understandable instructions for its use and very clear warnings about unauthorized reproduction.

Why Use an AIA Agreement Form?

Why reinvent the wheel? There will certainly be more stipulations and contingencies covered than you would think of and more than you'll conceivably use unless you run into trouble. And that is why it is a good idea to use them. There are very few situations you might encounter that are not covered by a definition, a way to determine responsibility, and an explanation of who has to do what. If you can't come to an understanding, the forms invariably include a section in which the parties agree to go to arbitration.

CHAPTER
5

Financing: Where Will the Money Come From?

Before you start tearing out walls, you'd better find out if you're going to be able to afford this venture. If you have just come into a sizable inheritance or won the lottery, you're in great shape. If not, you're going to need some financing. Your options here, like everything we've discussed up to now, should be explored during the planning phase.

How Much Is Enough?

Before you head for your bank to apply for a mortgage, you should have a good idea of how much money you will need. If you have gathered bids from contractors, you have a good starting place, but keep in mind that just about every remodeling job goes over budget. The scope and complexity of your project and the thoroughness of your planning will help determine how accurate you are in estimating your financial needs, but in any case you need to be alert to the likelihood of cost overruns. If you find as the job progresses that you need more financing, you can always go back for more. The frustrating part about needing additional funds, however, is having to reopen negotiations with the bank to cover those costs.

One architect I interviewed told me that he sends ninety clients out of a hundred back for more money after their jobs are partially completed. In his view the best way to anticipate your needs is to add at least 20 percent to your contractor's bid right off the bat.

Architect: *You have to be realistic about your budgets, and when you go for a loan, ask for 20 percent more financing than you think you will need. If you're going for a home-equity line of credit, go for 150 percent of what you think you will need. You only pay interest on what you actually use and you won't have to go through the whole process again if you underestimate.*

The bankers I talked to tended to agree.

Bank Branch VP: *In our experience two out of every ten homeowners who request loans for remodeling come back for more funds. We have learned to talk to them and gently push them to arrange for more financing than the bids they have received appear to call for.*

Banker: *Homeowners hardly ever ask for enough money to cover the cost of their remodeling project, which is inevitably greater than they were led to believe it would be when they applied for their loan. I would recommend that homeowners apply for 20 percent to 30 percent more than they think they'll need. If they don't need it, they can use it for other items they need or, better yet, leave it in the bank.*

That makes sense to me as long as you don't get carried away and begin to think anything left over is free money. It isn't; so don't.

Three Basic Mortgaging Approaches

If you think picking out wallpaper is daunting, wait until you see the array of mortgages and payment methods available to you. You can apply for a second mortgage or a home-improvement loan, negotiate an equity line of credit mortgage, or completely refinance your home for enough money to pay off your old mortgage and cover your remodeling expenses. The best approach for you will depend on a great many variables that involve your present situation, your future plans, and the state of the financial market at the time you apply for your loan.

When to Use a Home Improvement Loan

The banks regard a second mortgage or home improvement loan like a personal loan. It has a higher interest rate than an equity loan, must be paid off more quickly (usually in five years), and has an upper limit of $10,000 or less, depending on the bank. The only real advantage is that it is simpler to apply for and doesn't require the payment of points or, with some banks, any closing costs.

A home improvement loan might make sense as a quick source of funds for a small project such as a half bath, a deck, or some basic cosmetic improvements, particularly if you are doing the work in anticipation of selling your home soon.

Equity Loans and Equity Line of Credit Mortgages

If your project is going to cost more than $10,000, using your home as equity to finance your remodeling is a sound approach to obtaining funds. With an equity loan all the funds are transferred to your account, and you start paying on the principle and interest from the date the transfer occurs. With an equity line of credit, your bank opens a separate account for the funds you have contracted for and issues you a checkbook so that you can draw on these funds as you need them. You pay interest only on the funds you spend. Since remodeling projects often extend over several months, considerable interest expenses can be saved with this method. It also allows you to line up sufficient extra funds to handle the inevitable cost overruns without having to renegotiate another loan or pay interest on funds you don't need.

You can set up an equity line of credit mortgage well in advance of your actual need, and the bank will reserve the funds and wait for you to withdraw them. You can draw against the fund for up to ten years, and repayment must be completed within an additional ten years.

Since you are borrowing against your home, the interest on your equity loan and line of credit, even if you use the funds for a car or other personal uses, is tax deductible. Your bank may charge you an annual service fee in the fifty-dollar range for each year you do not actually draw any of the funds.

Refinancing Your Mortgage

If you expect your project to run over $10,000, it will probably take your loan application beyond the range of an equity loan or second mortgage. Assuming there is sufficient value in your house beyond its present mortgage or that the remodeling project will increase the value of the property enough to meet your bank's mortgage requirements, you should probably apply for a new mortgage for an amount that will pay off the original mortgage and cover the cost of your remodeling plans.

Not too many years ago, most people had a friendly local bank where they did all their business. They knew their banker and their banker knew them. A mortgage agreement felt more like a formality than a necessity. Things have changed. Even if you still have a friendly local bank and a banker who knows you, the chances are the bank will resell your mortgage to a government program such as Ginny Mae, an insurance company, or some other private mortgage company. All such mortgage purchasers require detailed information about your financial history and you to meet fairly stringent guidelines.

Bank Loan Rules of Thumb

If you remember what it took to get the mortgage you now have, it won't surprise you to learn that refinancing your mortgage is still among the most labor-intensive tasks you will face. To qualify for a refinancing mortgage large enough to pay off your original mortgage *and* cover your remodeling, you must prove to the bank that you are in a position to pay it back. To increase their chances of making a valid loan, bankers have come up with some rule-of-thumb ratios to size you up.

- Your monthly payments on the PITI (Principle & Interest + Taxes & Insurance) on the *proposed* mortgage should not exceed 28 percent of your monthly income. As a formula this would be: Your monthly housing expenses divided by your monthly gross income = 28 percent or less.
- Your PITI plus all your other monthly debt payments (other mortgages, credit cards, auto and other loans, etc.) should not exceed 36 percent of your monthly income. As a formula this would be: Your total monthly debt payments + PITI divided by your gross monthly income = 36 percent or less.
- You are a somewhat more attractive prospect if your original mortgage plus your remodeling loan total is under $202,301, as your bank can easily "sell" your mortgage to a variety of mortgage investment companies as well a couple of federal loan programs.

The variables you bring to the equation include:

- how much equity (the difference between your home's current value and the amount you still owe) you have built up in your home;
- your current income and expenses;
- the assessed value of your home;
- the total amount of the mortgage requested;
- how long you plan to own the house; and
- your willingness to gamble on future rates.

If you bought your home before housing prices began to soar in the 1980s, your appreciated real estate value may give you enough equity in the house to make getting a loan comparatively easy.

Banker: *Ninety percent of the homeowners who come in for a loan for remodeling sail right though the process. It's the remaining 10 percent who may be biting off just a little more than they can chew that require more creativity.*

Homeowner: *We used a variety of approaches. For the kitchen we just wrote checks as we went. We created the office with a home equity loan. But the next job, which involves enlarging the living room, will take a whole new mortgage.*

Sorting through Your Options

Most of us still think a mortgage means a fixed rate and thirty years. This sort of mortgage is still available, of course, but there are hundreds of other options available today, options that literally change from day to day.

Bank Loan Officer: *People come in for a mortgage with their minds already set on a fixed-rate, thirty year mortgage. I tell them I can arrange that for them but not before I learn more about their particular circumstances and not before I have had a chance to take them through some of the mortgage options that are available now. All I ask is that they keep an open mind.*

If you have your heart set on a fixed-rate mortgage, your bank has charts to help you calculate your monthly payments for interest rates, ranging from 6 to 17 percent for fifteen or thirty years. The rates are based on units of $1,000. You multiply the number of units you are borrowing by the interest rate you negotiate by the number of years of the mortgage. For example:

Rate %	15 Years	30 Years
8.25%	$ 9.71/mo.	$7.52/mo.
10.25%	$10.90/mo.	$8.78/mo.

The principal and interest payments on a $90,000 loan at 10.25 percent for fifteen years are 90 x $10.90 = $981.00 per month. To calculate your annual payments, multiply the monthly payment by twelve. You can see how much you will be paying in total by multiplying the annual figure by fifteen, but that will only make you unhappy.

Many people feel most comfortable with fixed-rate loans, but with the number of adjustable-rate mortgages (or ARMs) on the market, it pays to be open minded. After all, ARMs usually offer a lower initial interest rate, which may help you qualify for a larger mortgage. Keep in mind, though, that the interest rate on an ARM is pegged to one of several market indexes and thus may go up or down. Because payments change, ARMs are best for young homeowners whose income is growing or for people who expect to move frequently.

On any given day at the bank, you may be able to choose among the following mortgages:

- a thirty-year fixed-rate mortgage;
- a twenty-year fixed-rate mortgage;
- a fifteen-year fixed-rate mortgage;
- a capped convertible one-year adjustable rate (2+6) mortgage
  (Translation: Interest rates may go up no more than 2 percent a year, depending on the movement of a market index, and no more than 6 percent over the life of the mortgage. You have an annual option to lock in a current rate.); and
- A 5/25 balloon mortgage (Translation: a five-year fixed-rate mortgage with monthly payments equivalent to those on a thirty-year mortgage. You have an option to extend the mortgage twenty-five more years at the then-current rate at the end of the fifth year or pay off the entire balance by arranging a new loan.

One banker showed me two 6-inch-thick binders containing information on hundreds of mortgage programs from private mortgage lenders. There are also several government-sponsored programs available. It will be worth your while to sit down with your banker and learn more about them so you can find the best one for you.

Mortgage Brokers

Just check your Yellow Pages under Mortgages and you'll see that there are a number of alternative financing companies and services to choose from. These range from the local loan shark to very reputable nationwide companies. Many offer 800 numbers and could be worth an inquiry.

Mortgage brokers will be among those listed. They are usually unaffiliated with any one lender and have access to a variety of national or regional lending institutions as well as local banks. For a commission they will collect the necessary information from you and then try to place your mortgage with one of the companies they deal with. You could probably do as well as they do in your local area, but mortgage brokers working on a wider scale may be able to find more attractive terms for you. You'll only find out by talking to them.

Obtaining Financing

As you embark on your search for funds, keep the following points in mind, whether you are applying for a second mortgage or an equity loan, or trying to refinance your entire mortgage:

Obtaining Financing Takes Time

Getting remodeling financing, or any mortgage for that matter, seems to follow the same rule of thumb as construction: It takes three times as long and costs twice as much as you thought it would. My banker tells me second mortgages and equity loans might take a couple of weeks less time than refinancing.

Obtaining Financing Requires That You Scale a Mountain of Paperwork

When you apply for any of the remodeling financing options, your banker will treat you as if you were applying for your first mortgage. You'll have to jump through all the same hoops, so get your financial affairs in order before you go in.

Be prepared to provide copies of your income-tax statements for the last two years, proof of your salary from your employer, and a list of all your outstanding debts—i.e., automobile loans and outstanding credit-card balances. If possible, pay off those outstanding credit card balances; it will make your financial picture much brighter.

So that the bank can determine your ability to repay your loan, you'll also need to make another list of all your monthly housing expenses: current mortgage expenses (principle and interest), second mortgage expenses (if you have one), real-estate taxes, mortgage-insurance premiums, and your average monthly utility expenses.

Finally, in order to calculate your net worth, the bank will want a list of all your assets such as bank accounts, stocks and bonds, life insurance cash values, vested retirement funds, and the value of your autos, any businesses you own, and any other property you own.

Obtaining Financing Requires That You Find out the Market Value of Your Home

Most banks will only loan you between 75 and 85 percent of the appraised value of your home. The bank will conduct a formal appraisal of your home before it approves the loan. But if you think your financing needs are going to be close to the maximum, you can get some idea of what your home is worth by looking up the selling prices of comparable homes in your area. You can have a local real estate agent compile a list for you, or you can dig through the real estate transfer books at your town or city clerk's office. You might then offer your list of "comps" to the bank's appraiser to save some time and give a slight edge to a higher valuation.

If you determine that you'll need more financing than the equity on your present home can justify for your remodeling project, ask your lender to loan you money based on the increased value that the remodeling will add to your home. You should be aware that your bank may not value your remodeling as highly as you do.

Banker: *Just because you spend $25,000 on remodeling your $100,000 home, the bank will not automatically appraise your house at $125,000. You're more likely to get full value for a new kitchen or bathroom, but the cost of a swimming pool, for instance, will add only a fraction of its cost to the appraised value.*

If you refinance and add in the remodeling costs, the bank will probably treat your project as it does new construction and hold a portion of your funds in escrow until it conducts a final appraisal after the work is "substantially completed." Only then will it release these funds.

Remodeling Loan Application Checklist:

- Best estimate of project cost + 20 percent
- Plans and remodeling contract (not required but will help loan officer understand your project)
- Contractor's name (The bank may know him and his reputation.)
- Copy of property survey
- Social Security number(s)
- Name and address of employer for past two years
- Present annual family income (If self-employed, last two years' tax returns)
- Name, address, account numbers, and balances for all bank accounts.
- Listing of assets, including life insurance, stocks, bonds, autos, other property, other assets
- Your attorney's name and address

Choosing a Bank or Lender

Unless the recent recession has caused a revolution in the banking business, I'm afraid you will learn to heartily dislike bankers and the lending process in general by the time you close. I know we did. Much like a politician running for office, the banker we finally chose was able to tick off all the problems we were having with other banks—red tape, can't reach your loan officer on the phone, long delays, layers of extra charges, appraisals. He knew them all and even assured us we would be able to call him day or night; so we went with him and his bank.

It's no wonder he knew the problems; his bank still had them all. Yes, we were able to call him day or night . . . he had an answering machine. I guess he hadn't actually said we would actually be able to *talk* to him. Somewhere in the middle of the loan process, he disappeared. As a parting gift he miscalculated the amount we would need to pay off the old mortgage and finance the remodel, underestimating it by $10,000.

Before he left our banker extraordinaire set up a bridge loan. This is a very short-term loan you get to tide you over until you get a real loan. The bridge loan made it possible for us to meet the first installment due our builder more or less on time, but it so muddied the financial waters that we didn't know we hadn't borrowed enough until well after the closing. We couldn't figure where we had misplaced $10,000. We have since borrowed that missing amount, but it's not part of the mortgage so its annual interest is not a deductible expense even though it is for the house.

My recommendation is that you balance facts against gut feelings when selecting a bank or lender. To put it differently, a good loan officer may be more of an asset in the long term than a rock-bottom rate. Going for the absolutely lowest rate isn't very different from automatically accepting the lowest bidder as your contractor. You could be asking for trouble: Delays, mistakes, and inaccessibility are all too common.

Banker: *I find that applicants come in armed with all the latest interest rates and are looking for the absolutely lowest rate. This is understandable, but I also suggest they look for a loan officer that they like, one who is able to explain the vast number of options available, is willing to work with them as they prepare their application, and who will see them through the lengthy process.*

Additional Costs You Can Anticipate

Once you've lined up your refinancing loan, you can anticipate paying from 3 to 4½ percent on top of the amount in closing costs and other fees. By law your bank must furnish you a "good faith estimate" of your closing costs. (Some banks do not charge any closing costs for equity loans and second mortgages. Others do.)

Some of those expenses include:

Points. Usually one or two, representing 1 or 2 percent of the total value of your mortgage, which your bank charges you up front to take your business. On a $100,000 mortgage, this amounts to $1,000 or $2,000. In general, the more points you pay, the lower your rate will be. You can get a mortgage without paying any points at all, but it will be at a higher rate.

A rule of thumb for you: To justify the cost of paying two points up front to refinance a mortgage, you need a 2 percent reduction in your original mortgage rate, and you must plan to live in your house for five years. At that point the savings you've earned on the lower monthly mortgage payments over the five years will add up to the amount the two points cost you. From that point on you can actually call your refinancing a savings.

Attorney's fees. You or your bank must retain an attorney to search your title to make sure there are no liens or other encumbrances on it and to be present at the closing. My bank will accept my attorney, but some like to have their own attorney do the work. If you feel you need your own attorney also, you get to pay for them both. The estimate I got for this service was between $400 and $600. Working under the assumption that if there is only one attorney there will be less chance of a fight, I have always accepted the bank's attorney.

Title insurance. This is a one-time premium payment on insurance to protect the bank in the event its attorney missed something during his or her search. It can be between $500 and $600 on a $180,000 mortgage. You'll have to pay more if you want *your* interests insured.

Bank application fee. This is a fee charged by the bank to accept your application. Some banks will return this fee if they turn down your application. In our case the fee was $300. It is due when you submit your application.

Appraisal fee. This charge, which may vary from community to community, pays for a statement of your property's value by an independent appraiser or by a member of the lender's staff. In the past it was common practice to do a "drive by" appraisal, but now the firms purchasing mortgages want a formal appraisal. Cost: between $300 and $600.

Recording fees. This covers the cost of getting your loan on your town's books. Still a refreshingly small amount in most communities.

Remodeling with Less Money Than You Need

If you are long on projects for remodeling and short on money to do them all, here are some alternatives you might consider:

Do one project at a time. If you need a new kitchen and a new bath, and you want to enclose the porch to create a den, don't think you have to wait until you can finance the whole package. Since the kitchen and bath are the two most expensive rooms to remodel, start with the porch.

This means you will be an experienced remodeler by the time you get to the expensive projects. You will have tested a couple of contractors and some subcontractors under fire and learned how good or bad they really are, and you can use what you learned on the smaller jobs to do a more efficient job on the larger projects.

By doing one room at a time, you'll also be able to keep the disruption to a minimum. If your kitchen is out of commission, it's comforting to still have a viable bathroom. It's perfectly fine to wait to tear up your bathroom until your financial well refills.

Remodeling your home in a series of small steps is a very sensible approach, especially if you have more patience than money. It avoids the problem of making one big mistake that you'll have to live with for years. You can change contractors gracefully. You can learn from each project. One disadvantage is that you have to put up with all the disruptions, mess, etc. several times instead of just once and you may never get to subsequent projects.

Do part of the work yourself. I'm not talking about major carpentry or plumbing—I'm talking about opening a can of paint and priming and painting an inside wall or two. You might also sign up to do some of the things contractors hate to do, like sweeping and picking up at the end of each day, in return for some cost reduction.

A friend of mine in Vermont remodeled several houses and converted an old hotel into apartments. Each time he hired the same local seventy-year-old carpenter and served as his assistant. Although my friend was still in his forties, he had a hard time keeping up, but by the time they got to their third project, the old Vermonter figured my friend might almost be worth what he was writing off as his wages on the job.

Homeowner: *We had a contractor tear out our old kitchen, knock out a wall, and rebuild a larger room complete with electrical outlets, plumbing, and walls. I then took on the task of building the countertop and cabinets, putting in the sink and fixtures, laying the flooring, and doing all the papering and painting. It took a lot longer than I expected, and looking at it now, I can see all the mistakes I made, but it was all we could afford at the time. Seven years later, we extended the house, and this time we let the contractor do everything except the painting.*

The advantages to this approach are that you can save some money, get the project started a little sooner than if you have to wait until you can afford all the plans you have, and do a little pointing-with-pride at the finished project.

The disadvantage is that it could be years before you get around to doing your part. We tend to be more forgiving of ourselves than we are of the hired help; so, depending on how much of the project you take on, you could be living in quiet disruption for months or years.

You also need to be sure your contribution to the job is of a high enough quality that it doesn't detract from your contractor's hard work. Real estate people have told me of many instances in which a homeowner's handiwork has actually lowered the resale value of the house.

Obtain some unconventional financing. A New Yorker told me about yuppies rehabilitating their brownstones with their MasterCards. When they paid off the amounts they had charged, they would go out and buy some more materials. But it's not a joke and it's not limited to New York brownstones. I talked to several homeowners who had used the credit-card approach at some point in their projects. All you have to do is look at the annual interest rate on your credit-card balance to realize it's certainly not a sound financial approach. On the other hand, it's fast and you don't have to pay any points. Nonetheless, it makes more sense to pay cash as you go if you possibly can. When you have a little saved up, buy the materials and get started.

Consider alternative loan sources. Borrow from the folks or family. A business associate once advised me early in my career to beg, borrow, or steal to get a down payment on my first house as soon as possible. He had my family in mind for the first two approaches and didn't really mean the last. The same advice may apply to remodeling. Your folks or even your siblings might be very glad to advance you some cash for your project. I suggest you treat it as a loan and draw up a formal loan agreement with interest and a payment schedule to keep misunderstandings to a minimum.

Homeowner: *We sold stock, borrowed from her parents, my parents. We also had an uncle who had recently died, and the prospects of an inheritance gave us the final push. His estate, however, wasn't settled until six years later . . . and we were depending on that money. We did manage things so all the costs of the renovation were able to be written off as an investment because we did not live in the building and we were creating apartments.*

Barter is another approach that has been used successfully. A lawyer, dentist, doctor, or accountant might have a better chance of working out a barter arrangement with a contractor than a mortician or the manager of a dog food factory, but the idea is to trade services or goods instead of money for building services and materials. You'll need your accountant to explain the tax implications of this method of exchange. The IRS is interested.

Where Does All the Money Go?

I like to think that if you follow the suggestions in the first four chapters, your contract will be accurate and complete, your contractor will be experienced, capable, and honest, and your project will have a better chance of coming in on bid than the average remodeling project. But I don't want to mislead you. Even if you, your architect, and your contractor have all done your homework, the chances are good that your remodeling job will cost at least 20 to 30 percent more than you expected. In this chapter we'll explore why things go wrong, where overruns are most likely to occur, and how you can avoid them or at least keep them to a minimum.

Our Experience

Our builder submitted a bid and contract that called for a total cost of $80,000 for the project. He agreed to let me act as a co-general contractor. As such I negotiated for the kitchen cabinets and their installation, got a good deal on all the framing lumber, and paid for both the cabinets and the lumber. During the job we found out we didn't have to buy a new furnace, which had been included in the original estimate. But did the contract price drop by the $13,000 that this discovery and my purchases saved? No.

Was I upset? Well, yes I was, until I remembered that after our contractor's initial bid, we decided to add 2 feet to the back of the house beyond the original addition. (That's 30 feet by 2 feet on two floors.) We discovered that the cement slab of our front porch was cracking, so the contractor tore up the old cement and built a new wood porch with a wooden railing. I don't know what these changes were worth, but did the contract price go up? No.

Eileen and I said at the beginning that we would do all the interior painting. We didn't do any, but the price stayed the same. Did we get taken? We don't think so, and we invited our builder to our wedding a month later on the new lawn he promised would be there.

Whereas our costs and savings went both ways, most homeowners find that the ratchet only goes up from that winning low bid. If your contractor left major items out of the estimate and/or made piddling little allowances for fixtures, cabinets, floor and wall coverings, and appliances, your costs will go up when you hit the showrooms and select the things you actually want to live with.

Where Cost Overruns Occur

Behind the Walls and Under the House

Surprises can lurk behind your walls. Remember the builder mentioned in chapter 3 who found that all the wiring in the house ran down through the wall he thought would only cost a couple hundred dollars to remove? All that wiring not only had to be rerouted but replaced with wiring that met today's codes.

Most builders, and certainly the one you have hired, will know which walls are weight-bearing. If your plans call for a large opening in a weight-bearing wall or a weight-bearing wall to be removed, heavier vertical structural members will be needed, and additional wood or even a steel I beam will be necessary to carry the weight across the span. If this comes as a surprise and increases the cost of the job, you are in the wrong hands.

Subtler surprises are common as well—for example, plumbing lines that show up in the space where you wanted a window or abandoned chimneys and brick walls that have been covered over and will have to be removed at extra cost. But the main culprit, the one that is hardest to predict, is dry-rotted or water damaged wood. When you find this where you expected to find sound material on which to build, you suddenly have a project that requires rebuilding, not just redecorating.

Among the people I talked to, the couple that had the largest cost overrun started with a project calling for a new set of stairs to a remodeled master bedroom and an 8-foot, two-story addition off the side of their 1700s seaside cape. The addition was to house a small library on the first floor and two new bathrooms on the second. The project went to $140,000 from an initial estimate of $25,000 and took nine months instead of four to complete.

Homeowner: *Every day held a new surprise. When the builder took out the back stairway to the second floor and checked the wall behind it, he found that all the nails holding the studs to the beams and the siding to the studs were rusted off. The builder figured the only thing holding the back wall on was the paint. All the siding had to removed, not only from the back wall where we first found the problem but from both sides of the house as well. The studs had to be renailed and all new siding installed. The only good thing about it was it made it easier to decide to put in two new picture windows.*

Theirs was a classic remodeling of an old house. Every time the builder uncovered some part of the house, an additional project was created. The entire sill, huge 12-by-14-inch timbers, had dry rot and had to be replaced. The floorboards of one of the first floor rooms were no longer attached to the floor joists and also had to be replaced.

Fortunately, this particular couple could afford the additional cost, and the prime seaside location certainly justified it, but to most homeowners an increase of 600 percent over the original bid would be a disaster.

Underground

The majority of cost overruns that come to light when the shovels hit the backyard fall into three categories: ledge, water, and septic systems. Ledge changes a digging project into a blasting or drilling job, and the costs go up accordingly. If you hit groundwater or the water table within a couple of feet, your basement and foundation become a major project, and a conventional septic tank is virtually out of the question. Meanwhile, costs for installing or moving a septic system can easily rise if you get bad results from your percolation test, which measures the time it takes water to seep out of a hole and is often required by the health department. If the test reveals clay instead of friendly gravel, your septic system can become a major expense. If the odds are truly against you, you can have a 2-foot water table and still need a 1,000-foot well.

In the Contract

If you have read other books and articles on remodeling, you've no doubt encountered authors who advocate the fixed- or firm-price contract (or *stipulated-sum* contract as it is sometimes called), over the cost-plus type.

I tend to agree with these authors on the advantages and dangers of the cost-plus type, but I disagree with their assessment of the lack of risk to the homeowner in the fixed-price contract. The way they see it, a fixed-price contract forces a contractor to eat the cost increases that occur if he encounters an unexpected number of surprises.

I beg to differ. My interviews with contractors indicate that they have recognized this risk for some time and have worked out ways to lessen it that are written right into that "firm" contract, as I showed in the sample kitchen remodeling proposal in chapter 4. The design/remodeling firm that supplied this example is highly reputable, yet, as you saw, their "firm" bid could well be $10,000 less than the eventual cost to the homeowner when all the appliances, decorating costs, electrical fixtures, and any surprises are added in. It happens . . . frequently.

At City Hall

Another actor hiding in the wings who might have some costly surprises for you is your local building inspector. You may be happy with the old electrical panel in the basement, and you may even convince your contractor that a few more circuits will work fine, but the inspector is looking for building-code violations, and he or she may require you to buy a new, larger electrical panel and replace all the old knob and tube wiring in your house before giving you your certificate of occupancy. Needless to say, this kind of surprise can easily short-circuit your budget. You either comply with the inspector's demands or you don't move in.

In the Showroom

You and your spouse may be the reason your costs go up. If one or both of you have adopted the philosophy of "We only get to do this once in our lives and we deserve the best" or "We can spread the payments for this over thirty years and won't even feel it," you are in for a serious shock. If you decide to go for the $1,200 gold-plated bathtub fixtures, they will cost you about $3,600 over the thirty years of your mortgage. Unless, of course, they break.

During the course of our project, like so many homeowners, we upgraded occasionally. For one thing, we decided to go with small-pane windows, or *true divided lights,* instead of snap-in inserts. And we had a lot of windows. Then my wife decided that the big picture windows in the original livingroom should also be true divided lights. (This wasn't an upgrade. It was a whole new idea.) Wouldn't those easy snap-in mullions be just as good, as our builder and I suggested? No! We even installed them. But three months after the rest of the house was complete, our contractor and his lead carpenter came back and installed the new true-divided-light picture windows in the living room when the order finally arrived. This did not come under the original bid, needless to say.

You don't have to buy fancy fixtures to have your bathroom costs go out of sight. If your plumber finds galvanized pipes behind the walls, he will probably talk to you about their remaining life expectancy and recommend strongly that they be replaced with copper, along with all the old valves and connections.

How to Avoid Cost Overruns

Develop a Well-thought-out Plan— and Stick to It

The best way to avoid cost overruns is to have a well-thought-out plan backed up with detailed working drawings. Then stick to that plan and keep your changes to a minimum. If changes to the plan are called for, try to anticipate them. Visit the work site every day, and if you see something that looks wrong or gives you some doubts, talk to your contractor and get it taken care of before he or she has it built and has to rip it out to make the change.

Don't Make Changes

The main reason I started this book with a chapter on planning is because lack of thorough planning, with the changes and mistakes that result, is probably the major contributor to cost overruns. Don't hesitate to change something if you see that it will make your house better, but remind yourself occasionally that doing a job over two or three times costs more than doing it right once, and it takes the heart out of your crew.

Investigate During the Planning Stage

You might let your contractor open up the walls in question and see what lies in wait for her before she submits her bid. Sometimes just the age of your house will alert an experienced remodeler to likely problems. Copper piping became the standard after WW II, but before that, brass, galvanized steel, and even lead were commonly used.

Do Some Tests in Your Backyard

Underground surprises are some of the most expensive. If you *really* want to know if the soil can handle your septic system or if there is ledge where you want to put your new footings, dig a hole where your foundation will go in and see if you hit ledge. If moving the septic tank is called for, do a percolation test in the area where it's going to go. Dig a 3-foot hole with a posthole digger, fill it with water, and time how long it takes to empty. Do it a couple of times in a row. Take notes. You may not know what they mean but the septic-tank people will.

Stick to Your Budget

Your contractor could come in right on bid and you could still be thousands of dollars over budget because you fell in love with the top-of-the-line items in the showrooms. Price the items you will need during your planning stage, put them in the budget, and stick to it.

Why Costs Go up Fast and Come down Slowly

Several of the homeowners I spoke with noted one of the construction industry's great mysteries: Costs can escalate in the blink of an eye, but they never drop as quickly when projects are scaled back. Why doesn't an 8-by-10-foot deck cost half as much as a 16-by-10-foot deck? Why does leaving an attic space or bathroom "unfinished" seem to save so little over the "finished" cost?

Contractor: *It takes just as many tools to do the smaller job. It takes just as long to set up and break down each day. And every board, no matter how long or how short, has to be cut once and nailed at each end.*

Contractor: *Whether you paint all day or touch up one window, if you open a can of paint, it has to be stirred, and it takes just as long to clean a brush after ten minutes' use as it does at the end of a full day. The more productive time you can allow between the setup and the pack-up, the more efficient the job will be.*

Would Keeping Track of Costs Help?

A normal business starts with a plan or business proposal, followed by a budget that lists estimated costs for raw materials, labor, and operating and overhead expenses. As the business goes forward, reports are usually generated in which the actual costs for each item are listed opposite the estimated cost, making comparison simple. You know when you are running over in some part of the business and are able to make adjustments or negotiate a loan for additional funds.

The same is not true for even a moderately complex remodeling. A majority of the materials and supplies will be ordered and paid for within a few days of the start of a project. The first load from the lumberyard will contain everything from the dimensional lumber, nails, Sheetrock, underlayment, and the flooring for the whole job to the many items for individual parts of the project such as tiles, grout, roofing shingles, and doors. The contract will have listed the materials for each room, and it's almost impossible to attribute each part of the load to the proper room.

How does a homeowner keep track of the costs on a remodeling project? There isn't any way. When it came time for me to write the first of the many checks to my builder, he turned over all his receipts for materials and supplies, his time cards and bills for the subs and their materials and supplies, and a total. I'm sure it was all there, but without reconstructing his entire business, there was no way I could know whether the estimated times and costs itemized in the contract bore any resemblance to this wrinkled pile of real life. Fortunately, I came to this conclusion very early in the project and didn't spend hours trying.

When I asked builders and contractors how homeowners should keep track of costs as the job progresses, I began to think my approach—in other words, of choosing the right contractor and then simply writing the check, with few or no questions asked—was the right one.

Contractor: *There is no way you can compare the estimate with the actual job. The fact of the matter is, the job should feel right to you in your gut.*

Contractor: *You know what? As a contractor, I don't want to work for someone who doesn't trust me. At the end of the week, my subs tell me how much they have worked, my carpenters turn in their hours, I keep track of mine, and I turn them in to the client. I trust my subs and my crew. If I didn't I would have gotten rid of them a long time ago.*

CHAPTER 7

Where Does All the Time Go?

An inn owner told me the best story I ever heard about the time it takes to remodel. After not having the use of a downstairs bathroom for a month, she gave her carpenter a stern talking-to on one of the few days he showed up. "I thought you told me when you bid this job it would only take you seven days," she said. "That's right, I did," he replied. "But I didn't mean seven days in a row."

When I asked contractors to explain where all the time goes on a building project, I got dozens of answers, citing everything from natural phenomena and acts of God to human error and miscommunication. Their explanations should give you some appreciation of the problems they regularly encounter in the course of a remodel.

Weather Delays

If you are planning a remodeling project involving tearing off a roof or adding a foundation and a structure to the side, back, or front of your house, it's not hard to imagine the effect a prolonged rainy spell could have on your schedule. If, however, you're working under the happy assumption that you won't be affected by the weather because the remodeling you're doing is all inside, think again. What do you suppose happens when your contractor, who said he would start your job on August 1, gets delayed for three weeks by rain on the job he's doing before yours? Yes, it could delay your start by three weeks. He might also come to you and ask to start your project two weeks early.

Contractor: *In New England we get seventy-two days of rain a year. That's one out of every five days. If a contractor or a subcontractor gets three or four days of rain in a row, he will look for a small inside job, like remodeling your bathroom. But when the sun comes out he has a problem: Does he leave you without a toilet until it rains again or does he delay going back to the original job until the bathroom is done? Whatever he decides will cause problems somewhere, problems that ripple through the entire system.*

Contractor: *I lose three days for each day it rains because all the subs I have lined up have to be rescheduled.*

Contractor: *We're eternal optimists. We always think this is the job that will work perfectly, no mistakes, no problems, and all the subs will come when they say they will. And we always forget to allow for bad weather.*

Delivery Delays

Your first impression as you stroll through a lumberyard is that everything you could possibly need is stored there ready and waiting for your GC's order to send to your site. There is plenty of dimensional lumber, two-by-fours, two-by-sixes, plywood, Sheetrock, siding, roofing, cement blocks . . . the basic stuff. But you might notice that all the windows, kitchen cabinets, and bathroom vanities are in little display areas. They're there for you to browse through, select from, and order. The actual delivery time of the items you want can be anywhere from a few weeks to a couple of months. That's why you need to decide what you want as early as possible in the process. Otherwise, you could cause a halt to all work as your contractor and the subs wait for the windows or cabinets to arrive.

Contractor: *Your GC can't control the lead time necessary for special orders. Therefore, homeowners must make up their minds as early as possible in the remodeling process on such items as windows, cupboards, doors, and even some fixtures so they can be ordered and on the job site when needed. Windows, for instance, can take six to eight weeks for delivery or even twice that if it's the busy season.*

Scheduling Delays

I once asked a builder friend as we were sitting in a golf cart why contractors are still on the phone early mornings and until all hours of the night lining up the subs they need for the next day, what with all the computer scheduling programs and management techniques available. He proceeded to paint a fearsome picture of the ease with which the best-laid plans go awry.

Builder: *I used to wonder the same thing, so last year I spent January and February getting everything lined up to start a new house in March. I had met with all the zoning boards and planning commissions and gotten their approvals, I had lined up an excavator to dig the foundation, foundation people, framers, carpenters, and all the other trades with firm bids and dates to start each phase. Then it rained the week we were to dig the foundation, and the foundation guy couldn't get back to me for a month. I had to cancel everyone and start over. It was the worst job I ever tried to run. I went out and bought a four-wheel front-end-loader so now I can dig my own foundations when I want to. One problem solved, many to go.*

A general contractor has to allow for a frightening number of variables, many of which he can't control. Building a simple addition or a modest house can involve up to eighteen subcontractors, from the excavator to the landscaper. Many if not most of these subs cannot do their work until the sub ahead of them finishes. The framers can't frame until the foundation is in, plumbing and heating people have to wait for the framers, insulation goes in before the Sheetrock goes up, and the electrician must come both before and after the Sheetrockers.

Contractor: *If the job calls for eighteen subcontractors, and if all of them come within two days of the time you have scheduled them (and that is very good service), they will have added thirty-six days to the projected time. And this is not taking weather into account; this is just guys showing up about when they said they would several months before.*

One contractor described being a GC as trying to fight a war with a rented army. No matter how precise his schedule, a GC can't *order* a sub to be there. If a crew is shorthanded or a sub misses his arrival date, the job goes slower and tasks have to be assigned to fill the gap. Part of a GC's job is to keep a list of things that can be done to fill in those blanks in the schedule and keep his crew busy.

Finish-work Delays

One fall Sunday afternoon my wife and I were walking the dog past a neighbor's side lot and noticed a foundation for a new house. When we came by the next afternoon, the first floor was completely framed. But the speed at which the first few steps in new construction and remodeling are completed is misleading. Homeowners tend to think every phase will go as rapidly, but it doesn't happen that way.

Homeowner: *It doesn't take long to tear things apart. But even after the Sheetrock is up, the job isn't even half done. In fact, the closer you get to being done, the more detailed the work is and the longer it takes.*

When you get to the part where the work seems to slow to a crawl, you're at the finish carpentry stage. Finish carpenters are the high end of the woodworking trades, just a little short of cabinetmakers. There are fewer of them in the world, and probably no more than one or two will be left to finish your job. They come in when all the rough carpentry is done, the windows have been installed, the kitchen and bathroom cabinets are sitting in their shipping crates, and all the doors with their frames are leaning against rough openings. A finish carpenter is the one who puts in the baseboards, frames the windows, puts up that molding you finally decided on, installs the medicine cabinets, builds the shelving in all the closets, and hangs all the doors.

Every board that is installed has to be measured twice if the carpenter follows the old adage "measure twice and cut once," cut (often at an angle that has to be calculated), and nailed. Then the nail has to be set in a little deeper so it can be puttied by the painter. Even the sounds from your project will change. No more pneumatic hammers. The pounding will be slower, with long pauses between nails. The sound of the skill saw will be replaced by the shorter and sharper whine of the chop saw, the modern-day answer to the miter box. And speaking of costs, which we seem to be doing frequently, if you're sent out to pick up $1,000 worth of finish-grade lumber, moldings, baseboards, etc., you won't need any help carrying it to your car.

Delays Caused by Changes You Make

It seems that no matter how thoroughly you plan, lay things out on the floor, measure, and try to visualize the proposed space, it looks different when the walls are actually up and you can walk into it. Sometimes it looks better than you had hoped, but frequently you will realize you've made a mistake. The window should be bigger so you can look out at the view while standing up or sitting down, the kitchen would be more efficient if the sink were on the other wall, a door swings the wrong way, your bedroom closet is too small, and the guest room is too big. It's got to be changed. Don't feel bad. This happens more often than you'd think.

Architect: *Architects don't care if work has to be torn out and done again because they don't have an emotional attachment to the work. I am detached from the project even though I drew the lines there. I have walked into buildings I have designed, and the whole building is framed and the rooms are framed, and all of a sudden you say, "Wow! Wouldn't it be swell if we moved this wall over there or we had a big opening here?" The client sees the same thing and maybe the builder does, too. But the fact of the matter is, the builder has an emotional involvement in those walls where they are. After all, he has paid people to put them there.*

If you feel a change is necessary, talk it over with your contractor first. He may have some suggestions that will correct the problem without making drastic changes. But if he doesn't come up with anything quick and easy, be prepared for extra costs and a longer job. The original work has to be torn out, new materials ordered and delivered, and the job redone. This will take time. If the Sheetrockers were scheduled to start their work the next day, your contractor may be able to have them start in another room and hope he is done with the alteration before they get to the room in question. If not, he will have to cancel and try to get them again later. But they may not be available for another two weeks—if so, your project will have to wait.

If it is a window that has to be changed, you may have to reorder, and that could mean another six to eight weeks for delivery. The rest of your job will be done, but you'll have to live with plywood on your living-room wall until the new window is delivered to the lumberyard. Then you'll have to try to get the carpenters back to put the new window in. No one will be very happy by this time.

The effect of a change or a mistake on the length of time added to a project is directly proportional to how early you catch it. We walked into our house one evening after the crew had left for the day and noticed that there was an extra window in the kitchen. We were still in the framing stage, so all we saw was two-by-sixes with an extra two-foot-by-four-foot box in them. I met with the contractor the next morning. We went over the drawings to see how it had happened. (As it turned out, the framing carpenters had used some old drawings.) Correcting the problem was simple—the framing carpenters simply put a vertical two-by-six in the box to fill in the stud pattern. Additional time: about half an hour. The subs who installed the insulation later may have wondered what we were doing, but by catching the problem early we saved a lot of time and effort. Of course, if we hadn't caught the extra window, the cabinet installer certainly would have, since the space it occupied was where his cabinets were supposed to go.

There's another moral to this story: Don't leave old floor plans lying around. Get rid of them before someone accidentally picks them up and uses them.

Your Contractor's-got-to-make-a-living Delays

As much as you may like to think that your project is the most important one in the world—and as much as you are led to think that by your contractor—the fact is that your GC has to be lining up his next job while he is still on yours if he is to maintain a steady income. To do that he has to visit other homes, meet with the owners, and put together bids and proposals. Most of this will be done on his own time on weekends and evenings, but some day visits may be necessary. He may also have to bid on several jobs to get one.

You really don't have to worry, however, unless he starts the next job well before he has finished yours. Just when your job is getting to the time-consuming, detail-work phase, he will have his head in the first phases of the new project. It is a normal construction practice to leave one or two skilled finish carpenters on a site to finish up the first job and take the rest of the crew to the new one. But from your perspective, this creates a situation in which not only is the work more time consuming, but there are fewer people doing it. By this point you will have become much less sympathetic to your builder's problems, but it may help to know it is the nature of construction.

An overlapping job *can* be an advantage in that it gives your contractor and his crew somewhere to go when your cabinet order or a crucial subcontractor is a week late or weather shuts down your project for a few days. But it won't do a thing for your peace of mind.

Poof! Your Contractor Disappears

In every remodel, the day will come when no one shows up at your house. One day is not too alarming, but when it goes on for several days to a couple of weeks, you begin to panic. It is safe to bet that you will also not be able to reach anything but an answering machine at your builder's home. You start reading the obituary columns in the local paper. Then one morning you wake up to the sound of a power saw and hammers—they're back.

Many builders go into the business because they like the freedom from corporate constrictions. But unfortunately, they may exercise this freedom during your project. There are some dates you can count on being free from the sounds of building. Across the northern tier of the country, you can circle the dates of deer-hunting season because the guys will be gone. Some contractors will warn you but most won't—usually you're just expected to know they won't be there. There is a similar period in the spring when trout-fishing season opens, but that usually lasts just for a day or two.

Contractor: *Contractors and subs take vacations, too, just like the homeowner does. Six months ago when his wife bought the tickets for the trip to Bermuda, he had no idea he would be in the middle of your job when the time came. Builders like to take their vacations in the summer months, just like the rest of us. That is the best time, and it is when they have some money. In the winter months they might have some time but it's because they're unemployed.*

Builder: *Regular vacations do not exist in the construction industry; so we have to just take them, and it's always the wrong time. I tell my customers that my fishing season is from September 5 through October 15 and I will be gone. Some contractors don't tell their customers that. They just go.*

We can attest to that. Our builder took off for Florida in February for a week. There was no warning. He just disappeared. When he got back he explained that he didn't tell us because he thought we might worry about the job. Of course he was right. We did worry. We would rather have known what was going on.

One homeowner who encountered this same phenomenon sounded amazed and more than a little miffed when he observed, "The whole crew took off for a two-week vacation right in the middle of our job."

One contractor summed it up best: *We have learned that if we just take the time off, we get bitched at when we get back. If we play it straight and* tell *the client we're going on vacation, we get bitched at twice—before we go and after we get back. Most of us have decided once is enough.*

Of course, builders may disappear for other reasons. All the things that cause a normal person to take days off from work can also affect them. They get sick, they have to cope with family emergencies, they get bummed out and need to get away for a few days. More likely, though, your builder has gotten into a scheduling bind and spread himself too thin. Perhaps that special bay window that had to be sent back on the last job has finally come in. He will pull his men off your job to get that installed so the previous client will get off his back and pay the last 10 percent of the contract. (The same thing might happen to your bay window someday. At least it shows he has a sense of responsibility to his old jobs.)

Is there an answer to the disappearing-builder syndrome? Not really, but if you're aware that it can and does happen, you won't be shocked, and just maybe your builder will level with you so you can calculate the time more accurately.

Look at the bright side. You'll have some additional time to pick out all the things you have to pick out. And, unless they were so unkind as to leave with the water or electricity turned off, you can have a little peace and quiet for a while.

How to Minimize Delays If You're Acting as Your Own General Contractor

The best advice is not to cut your timing too close. If the electrician says he will need two days to do his work, allow four days. If he gets done early, it will give you time to think and plan for the next sub, to make sure the materials you will need are delivered, and to clean up your site. You can always check to see if the next guy can come sooner than scheduled, or better yet, take the family for a two-day vacation.

Relax (You Have No Choice)

It is a generally accepted fact that a construction job will take more time to complete than anyone said it would during the planning phase. As one contractor suggested, to be realistic you might add two days to the original time estimate for every subcontractor who will be working on your job. It'll take more time if rescheduling is necessary due to complications and delays occurring either on your job, on another job, or in the lives of your contractor or his subs.

Add in all the delays caused by late delivery of the things you've ordered, weather, surprises, changes, and mistakes both on your job and the jobs preceding yours, and it's no wonder that projects run over schedule. At least now you know why.

CHAPTER
8

How to Live with
a Remodeling Project
(or, Whose House Is It Anyway?)

When you take on a remodeling project, you are inviting a group of noisy, messy, destructive, and disruptive people to move in with you. Some homeowners move out until the dust settles. Others schedule their vacation time to coincide with those dire weeks when the water and electricity have to be off.

Staying put wasn't really an option in our case. The old house was going to be destroyed except for two rooms in the front. We happened to have a spare apartment—mine—fifteen minutes away. This meant we got to live in dust-free, quiet, comfortable surroundings while all the remodeling was going on, but we were still close enough to keep an eye on the day-to-day progress.

If you don't have the luxury of fleeing the scene and have to stay at home, as most people do, keep in mind that the contractor and his crew will be in your hair from 7:00 A.M. to 4:00 P.M., five or six days a week. You are going to have to learn to live together in chaos without getting unreasonable, because if you get unreasonable you will add time to the project and up its cost. Before you demand something from your builder, ask yourself who will be inconvenienced: you, the builder, or the builder *and* you? If the requests you make only inconvenience the builder, you are being unreasonable. If you make such requests often enough, you will also make it well-nigh impossible for him to do his job.

What is unreasonable? Well, it would be unreasonable for you to host your regular Thursday-morning bridge club with the construction crew there. It would also be unreasonable to ask the builders to watch your four-year-old child while you go out, and even worse to ask them to watch out for your kids while you're home. No, they can't unplug their power tools when they are not using them so your kid can play with them.

I realize there will be times when you'll be feeling pretty darn unreasonable, despite your very best efforts and intentions. It's no fun running to the neighbors to use the bathroom, trying to cook on a hot plate in the living room, having to brush plaster dust off everything you and the rest of the family intend to wear each morning, or feeling like an intruder in your own home. But remember that you're not alone. Most of the homeowners I spoke with didn't enjoy themselves much, either.

Contractor: *A homeowner should understand that in remodeling it generally gets a lot worse before it begins to get better. And then it will get worse again. No matter how much you pay your contractor, it's impossible not to generate plaster dust, sawdust, or any of a number of other inconveniences, especially if you are working on the infrastructure of a house, such as a kitchen or bathroom.*

One couple described living with their project as being in a state of flux. They lived from day to day as the contractor slowly eliminated basic conveniences such as their closets, the bathroom, and finally the kitchen.

Homeowners: *We'd move from room to room because most of the rooms were dismantled at one time or another. We used pipes strung across sawhorses for our clothes because we had no closets any more. The kids didn't have any closets, either. The baby's crib was always covered with sawdust and plaster. What a mess.*

Homeowner: *Oh God, it was awful. They had to break through the wall of the kitchen into the living room, and all the walls in the dining room, which we never used as a dining room, came out. We could take showers and sleep upstairs, but the whole downstairs was unlivable. We had a little child and it was yucky.*

Homeowner: *The crew would re–hook up the water and electricity before they left each day; so we always had the basic stuff in the evenings and mornings. But the refrigerator was in the living room for the duration of the project (a kitchen remodel) and the stove, too, for part of the time . . . We ate out a lot.*

Two years later we did my office, which was in the garage. Everything was neat and clean until the last moment when they came through the wall of the house.

Accept the fact that the builder and his crew are going to be your roommates for a few short weeks of your life, and remind yourself that for many, many years afterwards, you are going to enjoy what they have done.

Should You Move Far, Far Away?

Unless you have a very deep pocket, resist the temptation to flee the work site altogether. One couple who lived in Maine visited their daughter's family in California for two months, about half the time their contractor estimated it would take to put up the addition to their home. Their costs went up 600 percent, from $25,000 to $140,000. It certainly sounds nice to take off for a month or two, but if you're having extensive work done on your home, you really should be there at least once a day to check on what's going on.

 Homeowner: *After our experience with this project and all the little things that went wrong that we could have caught if we had been here, I would not recommend that a homeowner leave town for any extended period during a remodeling.*

Take a short vacation or find friends or family with whom you can stay when your house becomes unlivable. But don't disappear for weeks. Keep checking on the job.

Take Your Vacation

If you feel you must have a break from the chaos at home, consider going on a short vacation when your house is likely to be at its most unlivable.

 Homeowners: *We always had electricity and water in the kitchen and baths, except for about a ten-day period during which we took off for New Hampshire. We actually planned it that way. The kitchen was completed during that time, so we never had to wash our dishes in the bathtub or cook in the living room. Since the new kitchen was in a different location, all the plumbing was different, and for most of the time it was being built we still had the use of the old kitchen and its plumbing.*

Painless as this solution sounds, however, it doesn't always yield perfect results. This particular couple wasn't around to make any decisions or answer any questions as the work in the new kitchen progressed, and they never even got to meet the electrician who put a grounded plug 5½ feet up on a living-room wall because there wasn't room for it in the kitchen. It's probably just as well. The wife might have killed him.

How to Make Life Easier during a Remodel

Prepare Your Home in Advance

Clear the space where the remodeling is going to be done. If you're remodeling the kitchen, empty out all the shelves and cupboards. Since you will still have to prepare meals for the family, work out with your contractor how long you will have the use of your stove, refrigerator, and sink in the kitchen. Once your appliances need to be moved out, select a place where you can set them up temporarily and move your pots and pans there. Keep your dry cereals and canned goods in boxes where you can get at them. Be prepared to wash your dishes in the bathroom sink, possibly before you use them as well as after.

Make an effort to move *completely* out of any space where work will have to be done. If your bedroom is being remodeled, set up cots somewhere else. Don't try to move into and out of the work space every day. It doesn't work.

Your contractor will try to keep plaster dust, sawdust, and just plain dust from escaping to the rest of the house by hanging plastic sheeting or tarps over doorways and generally sealing off the area. Unfortunately, the contractor's efforts are likely to be as effective as your barber's to keep hairs from going down your neck.

Because dust particles will penetrate everything, it's a good idea to move any delicate computer, stereo, or photographic equipment out of the house or seal it completely in plastic garbage bags. You might also cut down on further cleanup time by sealing off open cupboards and bookcases and draping your furniture with plastic drop cloths, at least until you get home at night.

Change your life-style. If you are social animals, accept all invitations to dine out, but don't try to entertain anyone at your house until the house warming.

Set Aside Space for Your Contractor

Your house is your contractor's and crew's workplace. The more convenient and pleasant you make it for them, the happier they will be and the better the work they will do for you. To accomplish this you need to supply some basic necessities.

The first is space. To supply that, prepare to lose your garage. If you're smart, you'll give it to your contractor and let her store her tools and materials there or in your basement. One very good reason to do this is that if all her tools are at your place, she will keep coming back. On rainy days she will be there. It will also save her time and you money if she doesn't have to pack up and cart away all her tools every day and unpack them the next morning. Cater to her because the more convenient you make her work environment, the faster the job will go.

You'll also need to supply secure room for your contractor to store materials. Although it's not as common on a remodeling job as on a new construction site, theft of materials left outdoors can be a problem in even the best of neighborhoods.

Homeowner: *We hired a reliable plumbing contracting firm, but they sent out a new man on the first day they hired him. He worked one day, made a mess of what he was working on, and did not come to work again. The next morning all the copper piping was missing from the side lawn. We suspected the plumber himself, but if he didn't actually take it, he certainly neglected to secure the supplies.*

You'll save yourself a lot of grief if you convince yourself that the space where your contractor and her crew are working and the space where they store their tools and equipment is not part of your home any more. You may continue to pay the mortgage, but your contractor owns it for the duration of the job, and if she tells you to get out, get out.

Contractor: *Every one of us has tried to be nice, and it seems every time we're nice, it doesn't work. When I say I need your garage, I need your garage, even if it means your convertible sits out in the sleet. The alternative is to move a construction trailer onto your lawn and you pay me $400 a month rental and whatever it takes to reseed your lawn in the spring.*

Let Your Contractor Use the Phone

Another necessity you must supply is a telephone. Your contractor will have to check up on dozens of details during working hours, from deliveries of materials to the availability of subcontractors. If you're going to be at home during the day, you might even become your contractor's secretary and answering service. It will save her from climbing down off a ladder to answer the phone, and it will make you feel like part of the crew.

If you won't be home during the day, give her permission to answer the phone. This lets her get callbacks. Our builder and his crew got fairly good at taking messages for us. It may be a little startling to have your contractor tell you as you walk in that your aunt Millie's birthday party has been changed to Thursday, but it will make her job a lot easier if she knows she can pick up the phone when it rings. If you want, you can always tell the people who call you regularly during the day to call in the evening.

Let Your Contractor and Crew Use Your Bathroom

Most of the workers who come to your home will be courteous and polite and will try to watch their language when you're around. Other than ripping out your walls, they will behave like guests in your home. You, in turn, should act like a thoughtful host as well as an employer and consider the basic needs of your guests.

Contractor: *I remember one job I was on, I mentioned to the lady at the beginning of the second week, that I was thinking of changing the name of my company to Camel Construction. "Why?" she asked. "Because camels never have to drink, and they can go all day without going to the bathroom. We would like to use your bathroom and have a place to get some water." Two weeks and she never even thought to offer it.*

The first morning your contractor and her crew are on the job, show them what bathroom they can use and assure them you understand that some dirt will get tracked in and it's okay. Have some towels they can use.

In areas with a large immigrant population, some members of your contractor's crew may not speak English. This will make communication with the crew more difficult but even more necessary. You might arrange to have the directions covering their basic needs written in their language or, if you're taken by surprise, lead them on a pantomimed tour of your facilities.

Eileen and I didn't get much of an opportunity to act the good hosts since the water and electricity were shut off almost immediately. Our contractor rented a Port-o-John that filled the basic needs of the crew. The cost was included in our bill. These outhouses are available throughout the country, and if you really don't want the crew to trample the white shag rug in your bathroom, ask your contractor about renting one for the duration of your project.

Contractor: *One lady was upset because one of the subcontractors she hired (that's something I won't let happen again) messed up her bathroom, so she locked the door. The nearest bathroom was 4 miles down the road at a gas station. When her husband got home I told the guy, "You have two choices: Either I rebid the job because I did not anticipate the extra time and mileage or you unlock the bathroom." He unlocked the bathroom.*

Understand That the Construction Crew Needs to Eat

For people used to the power lunch or to working on a report right through lunchtime, seeing a bunch of guys having a picnic in the backyard at 11:30 in the morning can be disturbing. But remember, these people are doing actual physical labor. They are not loafing on the job; they need a rest and they need the energy that food and Coca-Cola can give.

If possible, offer space in your refrigerator for the crew's lunches and soft drinks, or better yet, keep a supply of fruit juice and soda there for their use. Tell them where they can get a drink of water and supply some glasses and coffee mugs.

Contractor: *Some homeowners give you the hose to drink out of, but most of the time you have to ask. It would be nice if the homeowner said, "Here is the bathroom, I put a pot of coffee on for you, and there is soda in the refrigerator." You know, the best customers to work for are the blue-collar people because they understand that good working conditions are important.*

You should also consider supplying coffee and doughnuts every morning. If you don't, your contractor's crew will send someone out to pick them up. Because they're all waiting to be jump-started by the coffee and sugar, no one will do a lick of work until the guy who went for the coffee is back. When he does come back, everyone will take a morning coffee break. Obviously, it is to your advantage to have a pot of coffee and a dozen doughnuts on hand.

Don't Keep Your Contractor Waiting

Don't keep your contractor waiting on your doorstep at seven o'clock in the morning with five people on his time clock because you overslept and you want to shower and dress before you let them in to do their work. That's crazy, and yet contractors and builders tell me it happens a lot. They also tell me that if it happens very often on a job, they build those delays right into the price.

Be Prepared to Adjust Your Attitude

After a few years, a good contractor can read people by the way the house looks when she walks in. If a house is immaculately clean, with dust covers on the furniture and shelves of dainty knickknacks, she knows she is in for problems about noise and dust. She can also read people by their attitude when they are talking to her. She can tell if you are one of those people who thinks anyone who works with her hands is less socially acceptable than a stockbroker. Contractors probably know more about human nature than clinical psychologists. Maybe it's because they get to see us under stress.

You might consider treating your contractor as a social equal. You won't have to pretend. Chances are she has an education and income equal to yours. She just prefers to work at a profession where she can see the results of her labors at the end of a week and not have a boss constantly looking over her shoulder.

Children and Remodeling

Kids think remodeling is great. All the dirt, torn-out walls, knocked-down doors, pounding hammers, whining power saws, and grown-ups running around in bib overalls creates a scene kids love. The term *attractive nuisance*, which insurance companies coined to describe such potentially dangerous amenities as backyard swimming pools, perfectly describes what remodeling is to kids. But the danger it presents to children goes beyond the obvious power tools and unfenced openings in the floor. OSHA regulations require carpenters to wear hard hats, ear protection, breathing masks, and safety goggles when performing certain tasks on the job. Your children don't have those protective devices, and if they did, they would probably be even more reluctant to wear them than the workers are.

The key is to devise an arrangement that will keep your kids out from under the crew's feet but still satisfy their desire to know what's going on.

Homeowner: *For our first job our daughter was young and went to stay with her grandmother during the remodeling of our downstairs. For the second job, the crew, who all had children of their own, treated her very well, but for the most part she stayed out of their way. When the crew went home they would leave a board and some nails for her to play with.*

Homeowner: *Through a series of seemingly endless delays, the remodeling job that was to take place in the late winter and spring while my kids were in school started on the first day of their summer vacation. The men were great. They were nice to the kids, answered their many questions patiently, and gave them little projects to work on. I tried to keep the children out of the way as much as I could, which wasn't easy because we were putting on an addition that involved their bedrooms and a family room off the kitchen. There just weren't many places to hide.*

If you permit your children in the building area, you put your builders, no matter how much they like kids, into the position of being the heavies.

Builder: *It's the customers' responsibility to protect their children. As careful as carpenters are, we can't be watching out for children and the safety of our crew as well. We wind up being a son-of-a-bitch to the kids because if we're nice they're underfoot.*

Builder: *One time I was working on the outside of a new addition and had a stack of 16-foot planks upended against the side of the house next to a window opening. A gust of wind hit them and the planks tipped over, sliding toward the opening like a guillotine. Just then a kid stuck his head out the hole. I thought he was going to lose his head. Kids just don't belong on a construction site; it's bad for my heart.*

How to Cope

As kind as your contractor and his crew may be to your kids, it's best to keep them as far away from the job as possible. Here are some ways to avoid confrontations between children and workers.

- Schedule the work during times when your children are in school.
- Put toddlers into day-care centers for the duration of construction.
- If you're remodeling during the summer, send your kids away to day camp, scout camp, or any of the hundreds of specialty camps available.
- Engage your parents to get to know their grandchildren.
- Take advantage of every invitation the kids get to play with neighbors and school friends or to sleep over at their houses.
- If all else fails, rig a gate between the kids and the workers so the children can see what is going on without being able to get in the way.
- Alternatively, when the workers stop for a break or lunch or leave for the day, take your children on a tour of the work area so they can see what is happening.
- And finally, don't ask the workers to alter their ways of working to accommodate your children.

Builder: *I had a mother tell me, "Don't leave your saw plugged in because my little boy likes to play with it." So I had to plug in the saw every time I wanted to use it.*

The best advice is to keep your children out of the way. No matter how permissive you are normally, firmly draw the line between your children and where the work is going on. It's too dangerous for all concerned. Your child will recover from a few harsh words sooner than he or she will grow a new hand.

CHAPTER 9

A Day in the Life of a Remodeling Project

Your crew will probably show up between seven and eight in the morning. Your job is to have all your morning routines out of the way by the time they get there. Your GC will go through his daily roll call to see who made it in and who overcelebrated the night before, and he will adjust the schedule accordingly.

The crew will spend the first half hour getting their tools out and hauling building materials to the work area. The GC will go over the work scheduled for the day and assign jobs. This is the time they send someone, usually the GC, out to get coffee and doughnuts if you haven't taken care of it.

If the electrical, plumbing, or heating subcontractor is scheduled, he will show up about the same time, and the GC will go over the details of the job with him. The subs tend to go about their tasks completely independent of the rest of the construction crew. They bring their own helpers and have their own schedules. It's conceivable that they could all be there at the same time, so don't be surprised if one day you see what looks like an army of people crawling all over your house.

The GC will stay around until everyone gets started and to answer any questions they may have. He usually has a lead carpenter on the job who will head the crew through the day. The lead carpenter is responsible for handling the parts of the job requiring the most skill, such as measuring and laying out room partitions according to the working drawings. It is his responsibility to solve all those little details that aren't covered in the plans and to make hundreds of decisions along the way as he creates the three-dimensional structure you had in mind.

Meanwhile, the GC is off to pick up the next load of supplies, or he is on the phone making sure they will be delivered on time. When he gets back he usually discovers that several problems or surprises have come up, and he confers with his crew on the best way to solve them. This is the point at which you may get a call at the office and a chance to vote.

The crew generally takes a half-hour break for lunch about 11:30 A.M. Then back to work. As it gets to about 3:00 P.M., they will start packing up their tools, get your place in some sort of order, and finally sweep up the area. This is no small chore, and there is usually a debate as to whose turn it is.

The GC is usually on hand at the end of day to check on the work done and to see what has to be ready for tomorrow. This is the best time for you to talk to him and get caught up on the day's activities and progress. It is also the time he should be pressuring you to get out to the showrooms and make those decisions you have to make (see the next chapter).

By about 4:10 P.M. the crew heads off to a local pub. The GC has a couple hours' more work ahead of him after he gets home, lining up the subs he needs for the next day or the next week.

The Construction Crew as Family

Your construction people are going to spend more time under your roof than you'd permit most of your relatives to, and, like fellow passengers on a small cruise ship, you're going to get to know them. The bigger the job, the better acquainted you'll become.

The typical construction crew usually includes at least one joker, one philosopher, and one straight-arrow who gets to be the butt of a running dialogue of comments and observations. Homeowners who have been on hand during the day report that listening in on their crew's conversations can be highly entertaining if not particularly instructive.

One of the laborers on the crew at our house brought his dog to work each day. The dog had a wonderful time chasing geese and swimming in the pond behind the house. When we discovered some tools missing from the job, the young man and his dog volunteered to sleep on a cot in our unheated house as a watchman. We found out later that his girlfriend had thrown him out and he needed a place to crash, so his offer served a couple of purposes.

The Building Inspectors

Although it isn't a daily occurrence, you can expect regular visits from the local building inspector. When a project reaches certain stages of construction, an inspector must be called in before the work can progress. If you're laying sewer or septic lines, for example, the local health inspector must inspect them before they are covered up. Electrical and plumbing lines must also be inspected before insulation and Sheetrock bury them, and most municipalities require a final inspection before a certificate of occupancy can be issued. A good building inspector will also drop in, unscheduled, a few times during a project. If you or your GC will take a few minutes to show him around, you may make yourself an ally instead of an enemy.

Homeowner: *I have noticed that building inspectors do not like to be ignored. They like to be received like guests when they show up, treated with respect, accompanied on their rounds, and listened to—very much like a normal human being. Apparently a lot of builders just tell the inspector to look around, and oddly enough, he finds things wrong. Generally, if your building inspector doesn't get your attention or your builder's this time, he has ways of getting it the next time he comes. After the first visit I made it a point to be home when the building inspector came to call, and after that we never had any major objections.*

Yes, there are some inspectors who overstep their responsibilities and become petty tyrants, but for most homeowners the building inspector is the last line of defense against an incompetent or corrupt builder. And for most builders he is the last line of defense against a homeowner who is encouraging him to short-circuit the codes. The inspector, and the building codes he is responsible for enforcing, have your best interests and safety at heart.

Contractor: *The building inspector can be a pain, but I am not above using him as the heavy and letting him break the news to the client that a new circuit panel is going to be needed, even though I may have known it all along.*

Our local building inspector pointed out the code requiring electrical outlets on the dining island in the kitchen, a nicety designed to protect homeowners against breaking their necks tripping over an electric cord draped from a counter electrical outlet to the pancake griddle on the island. We think kindly of him every time we have pancakes.

Developing a Working Relationship with Your GC

Just because you're living in the house where your contractor is working does not guarantee that the two of you will communicate well. You may leave before he gets there, or you may be wrapped up in the details of getting up, feeding the family, and organizing your own day. The first half hour on the job is a busy time for your contractor also, and he may not seem to have time to talk to you.

According to a management course I once taught, the definition of communication is the passing of information and understanding from one human being to another. Talking does not necessarily mean communication. Some homeowners admit they talked baseball and weather with their contractor but considered it in bad taste to discuss the job. If they got around to questioning some detail of the project or expressing a desire, they did it so obliquely that the contractor never got the message. Of course, they thought they had made themselves clear, and by the time the owner and the GC were actually communicating, they were shouting at each other. In order to maximize good will and minimize skirmishes, it pays to observe the following rules:

Be available during the day to talk. How much or how little time you should spend on the job site varies with the job. You shouldn't be forever hovering nervously in the background, clucking like a mother hen. But there are good reasons for you to be there occasionally. Decisions have to be made and problems solved as the job progresses. The more available you are, either in person or on the phone, the happier you'll be with the outcome.

So that your builder doesn't proceed blindly, it's important to leave your work number with him and make it clear that he's welcome to call you if he has any questions on the job. You might *insist* that he call you:

- if he is contemplating a change that will cost more than $25.00;
- if he is going to do something other than what is called for on the plans;
- when he uncovers a beam or a brick wall you may want to save;
- if he is going on vacation;
- if some material or fixture you are responsible for selecting is not delivered on time; or
- if there is some way you can help, or an important errand you can run.

It's a good idea to keep an extra set of drawings at your office so you can discuss changes and problems intelligently.

You'll also want to arrange to meet your contractor face to face at least once a week. This is often easier said than done. If you and your spouse work, you may both be gone before your contractor gets to the job, and he and his crew may be gone by the time you get home. In that case you'll need some flexibility in your schedule so that you can meet with him to discuss how the job is going and what the crew plans to do that day or week, and to find out which fixtures and materials you have to select and when they will be needed.

An even better approach is to meet with your builder before work begins each morning or after work ends each day. It keeps you informed but out of the way. It also gives you a chance to bring up any questions you may have about the job or to comment on the work that has been done. (It's perfectly alright to compliment him on the quality of the work if you like it!)

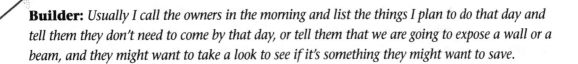

Homeowner: *It's tough when both husband and wife are working. We would see the contractor or his subs in the morning, and sometimes I would have to take off from work to find a fixture or some material I hadn't chosen. When we got home in the evening, we tried to take notes about things we saw that we wanted to talk about the next day with the GC. Or we'd leave a note. The workmen would call me at work occasionally. For instance, one day they called and said they had torn down one wall and found an old beam, and did I want to try to retain it. Sometimes we got a couple of days or a week to think about their question. Sometimes we'd have to make a decision over the phone based on their descriptions.*

A good builder will want to keep you informed and will work out his own routine for consulting you if you don't do it first.

Builder: *Usually I call the owners in the morning and list the things I plan to do that day and tell them they don't need to come by that day, or tell them that we are going to expose a wall or a beam, and they might want to take a look to see if it's something they might want to save.*

In general, a somewhat flexible schedule is a real asset during any remodeling project. If you can arrange at work to take off an occasional morning or afternoon to settle things on the site or to go on trips to the showrooms, your project will proceed with fewer hitches.

If you really want to get your contractor and his crew on your side, spring for lunch. You don't have to put on a tool belt and a baseball cap and try to be one of the guys (you'll never make it anyway), but if your office is close to your home, arrange to meet your contractor and his crew occasionally at lunchtime. Over lunch you have more time: You can talk baseball and still have time to communicate about the job. You don't have to be the center of attention, but you will be there as they discuss the problems they encountered and how they worked around them or solved them. You'll get a better appreciation of what goes into construction work. You may even pick up some ideas on how to make your project better. These are experts. They have seen lots of remodeling jobs and have worked in many other houses, so ask some questions.

I showed up a couple of times about an hour before lunchtime, offered to treat the crew to a couple of pizzas, took their orders, and went and picked them up along with some Cokes. (Save the six-pack of beer for an afternoon, quitting-time visit.) It was at one of those lunches that I learned they really liked the look of the home they were building. It made *me* feel good.

Architect: *I go in and sit down with the boys at lunch, and the communication is good and real. You learn a lot about what is going on with the job, and they learn a lot about why decisions were made. On one job the client made a point of coming to the site every Friday at lunchtime and bringing lunch for the crew. It would always be a gorgeous meal, and boy was that good for morale. It's a great thing to do and it's cheap.*

Not everyone feels comfortable hunkering down with their contractor and his crew. But the payoff can be considerable, as some homeowners I heard about discovered.

Architect: *I built a house for a very fussy couple who were both artists. They met with the GC every morning and were always around at lunch, and yet several mistakes were made due to botched communication. I asked them if they ever considered talking about the job at lunch when the whole crew was there. They thought that talking to the guys during their lunch would be a faux pas—that the only thing builders wanted to talk about was deer hunting and girls. They tried it and the results were amazing. They learned a lot about the job, and the crew learned they were actually pretty nice people to work for after all.*

Offer feedback regularly. If you have any managerial or child-raising experience, you know that people like to have their work recognized. The people remodeling your home are no exception. The first time I commented on the work of my crew was the time they took the chain saw to the back wall. After it dropped across the new foundation, we all walked out on it and I said, "Hey, great. You've given me a preview of the view I'll get from the deck when you're done." They laughed, and we began to get know one another better.

It may be difficult to find anything exciting to mention during the rough framing stage, but you can certainly comment on the amount of progress they've made, and if they have done a good job of sweeping up at the end of the day, tell them you appreciate it. Most people don't need any help finding fault and pointing out mistakes. That's a natural human trait. If a mistake has been made you should mention it, but try to temper these comments by letting them know when you think they have done good work also.

Builder: *I don't care what kind of contract I'm working under, I want some feedback. Do you like my work? Do you hate my work? People are terrible at letting you know how you are doing. Clients seem to be terrified of that. They're afraid of offending you, or looking naive.*

Take a diplomatic approach to problems. Don't save up your negative comments and observations and then dump them on your contractor all at once. That's a lousy way to start the day. Take a more diplomatic approach by asking questions such as "Does that banister look right to you?" or "Is there some law that says the bathroom vanity has to be knee-high to six footers?" or "How will we put furniture in the bedroom if the door swings that way?" You can still get your point across, but you'll be talking instead of screaming.

I have to admit that none of the homeowners I talked to took this approach, and none of the builders had encountered it. But it's the way I did business, and it worked for me. Our carpenter did some things for us that were truly creative, such as recognizing the potential and building a cathedral ceiling in the upstairs bath. I suspect he wouldn't have done that if we had been a pain.

Not commenting is another form of diplomacy well worth practicing. When Eileen and I walked into the new family room and saw 30 feet of oak flooring running in a different direction than we thought it would run, we didn't say anything. We hadn't actually discussed which way it would run and it was all done. We just stood and looked at it and slowly realized it really didn't make much difference. We could live with it . . . and we have. Complaining about it would have dimmed the crew's glow of accomplishment, and it wouldn't have gained us a thing.

Leave notes only as a last resort. If you and your contractor are like ships passing in the night, you may be tempted to leave notes stuck to the walls and counters. This is fine as long as you say things like "The cabinets look great. Nice job!" or "It's time to celebrate. I'll be by at noon with pepperoni pizzas for the crew." Otherwise forget it. There's nothing builders and their crews hate more than notes that say "Tear this out!" or "Wrong! Do over!" By and large, builders and their crew are in construction because they love it. Don't take all the fun out of it by leaving nasty notes.

Of course, if something looks wrong or you don't understand something, you can leave a friendly note inquiring about the item that perplexes you and asking the contractor to call you at the office when he gets in.

I know from experience that politeness pays off. Try it yourself and see.

CHAPTER
10

Decisions,
Decisions, Decisions

From the moment you decide to remodel to the first dust-free breath you draw in your new space, the most taxing, time-consuming, frustrating activity you will engage in is making choices . . . hundreds of choices.

You probably expect to choose the kitchen cabinets, the paint color for the walls, and the new appliances for your kitchen. You may also realize that you'll be called on to decide among wood, vinyl, ceramic tile, or linoleum for floors. But I doubt you're prepared for the literally thousands of options available, not to mention the range of prices. At first all stoves, faucets, and floor coverings look good. Then you learn about the advantages and disadvantages of each. After a few hours in a showroom, none of them looks good anymore because you have no idea how to decide among them.

Some Approaches
to Decision Making

Eileen and I went to only one floor-covering showroom, although if we had wanted to, we could have gone to six. It was late in our remodeling project, and we had already spent whole days in showrooms devoted to lighting fixtures, kitchen cabinets, plumbing fixtures, furniture, Oriental rugs, fabrics, paint, windows, doors, and hardware. We were beginning to get really tired of the whole process.

At some point during our shopping forays, I learned that we had a different outlook on the procurement process. To me, shopping was going out to buy something. To Eileen, shopping was shopping and buying was a separate process entirely, to be exercised only after a lot of shopping and not necessarily on the same day or even in the same week. Eventually, we worked out a system whereby she narrowed down the number of selections to a more manageable number by shopping before I got involved.

Perhaps the following strategies will help you make order out of chaos and protect your sanity and your marriage.

Do your research. Broaden your reading as you go through the housing magazines to include the advertisements and articles on lighting and bathroom fixtures, siding, roofing materials, items for the bathroom, and appliances. As you are planning, collect pictures of rooms that depict the style or feel you are trying to achieve. Try to come to a meeting of the minds on such things as window styles, types of flooring or floor coverings, kitchen and bathroom looks, and, of course, a budget philosophy.

It's not a bad idea to decide on some of the larger items during your planning phase. That way you can give a list of those items, along with style and model numbers, to your contractor. It's a good idea to collect the technical data sheets supplied by the manufacturer on your selections for your builder in case exact dimensions or installation information are needed.

Your GC should supply you with a long list of most of the things you'll have to select and should give you a series of deadlines for your decisions. You may have to make some decisions even before construction actually starts because some of the items you'll need—windows, doors, kitchen cabinets—are part of the basic structure and have to be ordered several weeks in advance so they'll arrive on time.

Keep ahead of the builder. You are part of the supply chain. If the builder starts to build the counters in your kitchen and you haven't picked the stove or refrigerator you want yet, work is stopped until you do. The electrical fixtures have to be on hand when the electrician is ready to install them or he'll have to come back. You can put off selecting the paint and carpets for a while, but the windows and doors have to be on site early in the process.

Know the lead times for delivery. Be aware of how far in advance you have to make your selections and put in your orders. Good intentions and bad performance will just add to the frustrations on the job. And remember to check delivery times while you're at the showrooms. The item you want may be on display, but chances are it still has to be ordered from a central warehouse or the manufacturer. Find out while you are there. Don't assume anything.

Know your budget numbers and allowances. In virtually every showroom you walk into, you'll find beautiful things that would be perfect for your home but cost ten times your allowance. As I warned you before, this is where you get the chance to blow your budget right out of the water. Know how much you can spend. Have it written down and stick to it, or at least stay within the total for a particular group of items. If you feel you really must spend an extra $200 for the light over the kitchen table, then spend $200 less on the recessed fixtures.

We used this approach with faucets. My wife made a trip to a specialty plumbing display room 50 miles away and came home with a $400 faucet set for the downstairs bathroom sink. It was the kind your folks probably took to the dump when they remodeled in the fifties, with four spokes and *hot* and *cold* written on the white porcelain centers. Even she was shocked by the price. We made up for it with $60 fake-brass faucet sets in the upstairs bath and kitchen. All of them turn the water on and off. (Ironically, guests compliment us far more often on the $60 sets than on the $400 job.)

Create and stick to a schedule. Choosing fixtures and so forth is a time-consuming process. You can't get it done in your spare time or when the mood strikes. Set time aside when you and your partner are both available and do it. Set up a schedule and stick to it. Take days off from work if necessary.

Comparison shop. This is easier to do at the beginning of your project than toward the end. It takes time and patience, and you may run short of both after a few weeks. Ask your contractor to recommend the showrooms you should visit. You can add to the list from the Yellow Pages. Showrooms tend to specialize in particular lines, and only by going to several will you be able to see the full range of what is available. Give yourselves the chance to compare not only quality and selection but prices. Get prices wherever you go. Let the salesperson know what your project is, and make it clear you're comparison shopping.

I can't honestly say we did this. We spent so much time debating which items to select at each place that we never got to other showrooms. We also did not get very good prices.

 Homeowners: *Our budget came into the decision process a lot. For instance, when we shopped for fabrics, we tried to select designs that were remnants or on their way out.*

Negotiate and bargain. To get a better price, it may not always be necessary to move down in quality. Most of the products you buy enjoy a comfortable markup, and you owe it to yourself to at least ask for a discount. You certainly won't get one if you don't ask for it. Call it a contractor's discount or a quantity discount, or, if you have been to other shops, call it an opportunity to meet the competition's offer. At the very least, you may get some additional benefit, like an upgrade on padding for your carpet for an average pad's price.

At the lighting showroom we selected all the fixtures we needed, and our contractor bought them on his account with his discount. Since we had arrived at a flat fee for his services, he agreed not to mark them up. Your contractor may not be so willing. But you can certainly discuss it with him during the contract phase.

Be willing to travel. You may know the way to all the malls within a 30-mile radius of your house, but chances are you have never been to most of the places you will have to visit to select the things for your project. They will probably not be in the best parts of town or even necessarily in your town. Expect to put a lot of mileage on your car during this effort.

In addition to visiting showrooms and display houses, you might also go through catalogues. We selected our toilets from a much-thumbed catalogue the plumbing subcontractor had in the back of his truck. The sinks came from a grubby little plumbing-supply house a friend of a friend knew about. Our old tub, we thought, looked just fine, so we moved it upstairs.

Many lumberyards display kitchens, baths, and certainly windows, trim, and moldings. Check them out as well.

Work out a system with your spouse. You and your spouse may start out by doing everything together: looking at all the selections, discussing the relative merits of each, and comparing prices. But sooner or later you may find that you have differing thresholds of pain. I found my nervous system couldn't tolerate more than an hour or two of "shopping," while my wife seemed to get stronger as she went.

I hit on a technique whereby she narrowed down our choices in a category to three to five fixtures or tiles or fabrics she could live with, and I selected among those. We each retained veto power over things we *really* didn't like.

Sometimes it becomes necessary to walk away from a decision rather than get into a confrontation. Go home or move on to another type of showroom, and let the decision percolate for a while. A fresh approach on another day can work wonders.

Homeowner: *I don't know whether it's simply out of exhaustion or what, but finally something clicks . . . a little light bulb goes off and you know you've made your decision.*

Some couples divide up the shopping duties, either because they lack time or because their interests differ. It's also perfectly okay to leave some things to your contractor's discretion. I chose one of our two toilet bowls (I went for a handicapped model that's a little taller—great for me, a surprise for our shorter guests) and let the plumber choose the second one. The shower heads were of particular interest to me, but we let the choice of the bath and shower faucets go to the contractor by default. We missed the deadline and something had to go in—right away!

Whatever method you use, agree on the approach you plan to take. Some husbands completely abdicate the selection process to their wives. That's not a good idea. In the first place, remodeling should be a joint venture, and choosing what goes into the home should be done by both parties. In the second place, most husbands find they have more opinions than they thought they had, if only financial. So they tend to second-guess their wives. That's a formula for trouble.

Homeowner: *My husband would send me out to pick out items and then criticize me for picking the most expensive. What I learned about him is that he does not like to make decisions, but he does like to second-guess other people's decisions. So I learned to narrow the choices down to two items: something I liked and something I didn't like. I would tell him I chose the one I didn't like, and he would always pick the opposite. So I got what I wanted and he got to overrule. Sometimes you have to do things like that.*

On the following pages are lists of some of the decisions you will have to make and some factors to take into consideration when making your choices.

Decisions, Decisions, Decisions: Room-by-room Checklist

Kitchen

The kitchen, along with the bathroom, is the most frequent starting place for home remodeling. It is also the most cost-intensive room because so much is compressed into a comparatively small space.

Cabinets: Your kitchen cabinets are the focal point of the room, so you want them to look good. They are also your storage facilities, so they have to be accessible and practical. You can buy made-to-order cabinets from numerous manufacturers. You can also pick out ready-made cabinets with enough different sizes to fit most needs. Or you can have a local carpenter or cabinetmaker build cabinets for you. Check out your options and the prices.

Our contractor calculated an allowance of $3,000 for cabinets, and he could have done it for that. Instead, we got solid cherry cabinets, listed at $18,000, at a 50 percent discount through a distributor who happened to be a client of mine.

Style: The choices are endless, as you know if you've leafed through a decorating magazine or strolled through a kitchen showroom lately. You can go for contemporary, traditional, or any of *many* available styles.

Open shelves and the country look are enjoying a comeback. You can opt for solid doors or for doors with glass fronts. We went with glass fronts with clip-in pane dividers for a restrained countryish look.

Special Designs: Gone are the days when kitchens were made up simply of upper and lower cabinets and drawers. Now, behind those cabinet doors are hidden specialty items: Carousel corner racks, slide-out shelves, pull-out garbage cans, tip-down scrub-brush racks, and, attached on the backs of doors, a wide array of special-sized wire storage racks. There are also so-called appliance garages—roll-front countertop storage areas meant to hide a food processor, a microwave, and so on. (We chose one to hide our bar area.)

Materials: Again, choices are vast. Cabinets can be made of wood (either solid or laminate, painted, natural, or stained), plastic laminate, or metal. Another option is to have a specialty firm come in and refinish your old cabinets. Such firms can provide a complete face-lift or just new doors. This is less costly than building new cabinets.

Hardware: This includes cabinet knobs, drawer pulls, and hinges. You have to decide whether you want flush doors with invisible hinges or hinges that will be part of the decor. The cabinet knobs—and there are hundreds to choose from—may seem like small items at $5 to $10 each, but when you have forty of them, as we did, it adds up. This was one of our toughest decisions, and we made it so late I had to install them all.

Countertops: Here is another area in which you'll be sorely tempted to go overboard. There are some beautiful new composites available, as well as the more traditional plastic laminate, ceramic tile, butcher block, and stainless steel. You can also mix surfaces—for example, by inserting a piece of butcher block in a counter finished in Formica. Faced with the vast selections and inflated claims of performance, it would be a good idea to ask your friends what kind of countertop materials they have, and how they like them.

Height of Countertops: The standard working height for countertops (and all sinks) is 36 inches. It hasn't changed since colonial times when the population must have averaged 5 feet tall. If you (and/or your spouse) are unusually short or tall, test various heights to see if another would be more comfortable for you. Ideally, you should be able to touch the bottom of the sink without bending over. But even if you're six feet nine, like my son, keep in mind that you may want to be able to sell your house to normal people some day.

Layout: My wife went through a mental dry run of baking a loaf of banana bread with our proposed kitchen layout in front of her. She reached for pans, mixing bowls, bread board, flour, spices, butter, electric mixer, etc., to see how well the kitchen worked. She also tested the direction the cabinet doors and the refrigerator door opened. And she mentally unpacked bags of groceries, unloaded the dishwasher, and cooked a meal. We ended up with an excellent layout, even though I've never seen a loaf of homemade banana bread since.

Appliances: You may want to pick a new color for your kitchen appliances. If you're going for all new gear, you'll have a chance to do this. Otherwise, match the appliances you are keeping. If both gas and electric hookups are available in your neighborhood, you can choose either for cooking. Then you will need to decide between a traditional range with burners on top and the oven on the bottom or a countertop range and a separate wall oven. Do you want a microwave oven built in as well, or perhaps one of those deluxe ovens that combines a conventional oven with a microwave? Other appliances you will need to choose include refrigerator, dishwasher, disposal, and trash compactor.

Location of special storage: Ideally, you planned for adequate storage while you were laying out your kitchen. You must now decide where you're going to keep all those small appliances you have or intend to buy: coffee maker, coffee grinder, food processor, toaster oven, toaster, can opener, electric mixer, hot plate, crock pot, radio, and TV. Then decide which ones you're going to leave plugged in on the counter and which will be stored. We put a few appliances out in full view and stored a few in big pull-out shelves behind cabinet doors.

Plumbing fixtures: Your major decision is to choose the sink or sinks you want. Do you want single, double, or triple bowls? Do you want a separate bar or vegetable sink on the island (if you have one)? Do you prefer stainless steel or porcelain? If you opt for the latter, you will have to choose a color. Remember that the sink will come with one, two, three, or four holes drilled in it for various faucet configurations and a hose. The faucets you choose have to match the number of holes in the sink. (Now is also a good time to decide if you want a water line to your refrigerator for an automatic ice maker.)

Bathroom

The bathroom has become the latest status symbol. People are spending thousands of dollars on raised whirlpool jet tubs overlooking panoramic views. If you think you'll really use some of this exotic equipment, by all means go for it. But remember that these special tubs are costly to buy, costly to install, costly to operate, and very costly to repair. You might check with people who have one and see how much they use it.

Plumbing fixtures: Bathtubs vary, from the traditional cast-iron tub on claw feet to near lap pools. Your choice of tub will dictate whether you want a shower in the tub or in a separate stall. Or perhaps you'll go for just a large stall shower. You'll also need to select a sink (or two if you're going for speed in the morning) and the toilet and its seat. You might also consider placing all these fixtures in separate rooms or compartments to allow for concurrent usage.

Cabinets: Bathroom vanities offer you the same options of design, style, and material as kitchen cabinets. You might consider a vanity with room for two sinks. It's also handy to have cabinet storage for towels in the bathroom.

Plumbing fittings: I chose our shower heads, and even my fussy father-in-law rates them a "ten." I also had them installed 7 feet up because of my height. (Tell your plumber where you want the shower head *before* he drills the hole in your shower stall.) In addition to the shower heads, you'll also need a set of faucets for the sink or sinks and the tub. Be sure to measure the distance between the outlet holes and buy faucets to fit, or if you selected the faucets first, buy sinks and a tub to match.

Another bathroom fixture you might consider, particularly if you have young men in the family, is a urinal. It lessens the need for accuracy and uses less water per flush than a toilet. Still another, since we're spending money on this bathroom, is a bidet, which is commonplace in Europe but much less common here. A friend with hemorrhoids says it's a blessing.

Miscellaneous: You will also need to choose towel racks, hooks, toilet paper holders, medicine cabinets, toothbrush holders, soap dishes, mirrors, exhaust fans, and perhaps an auxiliary heater and sunlamp. And now that you have this nice new room, you'll need towels, mats, and rugs to match plus a new shower curtain and new window curtains (or shades or blinds) as well.

Room-by-room Decision Checklist

On pages 126–27 is a checklist of some of the many basic decisions you will have to make for every room involved in your remodeling project. Each room may require additional decisions, depending on how you intend to use it. For example, a media center in a family room or a home office will require a whole separate checklist, but most of the decisions will involve specialized electronic equipment and the furniture you own or intend to purchase.

One important decision you need to make early in your project is whether you want your contractor to build in cabinets, bookshelves, work stations, and filing cabinets or whether you intend to go the stand-alone route. We did a little of both. We had the carpenter build a set of bookshelves into our master bedroom wall, but I built a tall country-style pine cabinet to house all the old hi-fi equipment and the TV and set it up in the family room. I have an office in my home, but the only special request I made to the contractor was for a dedicated electrical outlet for my computer.

The following checklist would have covered most of the decisions we had to make for all our rooms, including the family room and office. If you feel you need more details, attach a blank piece of paper to each copy of your checklist and add items as you think of them. You might also prepare yourself mentally for going over budget.

Keeping Track

One of the immutable laws of remodeling is that every decision you make leads to three more. If you decide to have tile instead of linoleum on the bathroom floor, for example, you will need to decide between plastic and ceramic tile, pick a pattern, and finally make sure your GC lays it out the correct way. We dropped the ball on the last step. The black diamonds–on–white squares pattern we selected became black squares–on–white diamonds when the contractor laid it out sideways. (If you want your tile to be laid out a certain way, be there when it's installed.)

When you add up all the decisions you have to make, multiply by the two or three showrooms you must visit to make each selection, add in the catalogues and advertisements you need to peruse, and multiply again by the number of people involved in making each decision, you can see that you'll have to devise a system of keeping track of where you've been and what you've seen, or you'll lose your mind.

My suggestion is an 8½" x 11" spiral notebook with three or four dividers and a heavy cardboard back. Use the first section to keep chronological notes on the job. Take notes at every meeting with your GC; record every telephone call (incoming and outgoing); note important names, addresses, and telephone numbers; date each page; and keep everything up to date.

Take the book with you when you hit the showrooms. Use the second section to draw sketches, collect pictures of different fixtures and appliances, and note the model numbers, styles, colors, and prices of the items you are considering. You can also staple in the business cards of any salespeople you meet.

In the back of the notebook, make a list of all the things you decide to buy. In the next column write down the estimated cost or the allowance your GC has given you for each item. In the third column note the amount you actually end up paying. Keep a running tally so you know how much you have spent. You may still go over your limit, but at least with this method it won't come as a surprise.

The loan officer of one of the banks I visited recently got all misty eyed when I told her I was writing a book on remodeling. It seems she had acted as her own GC on two major remodeling projects and loved it. She recalled that she still had a notebook she had compiled—"My personal Yellow Pages," she called it—with a complete history of what happened, when it happened, and who she got to do what.

Among all the decisions you will have to make lurk a few on which you and your spouse won't be able to agree. You both know you're right and the other one always spends too much money or has lousy taste. It's an impasse. In the next chapter you'll learn how other couples have avoided this pitfall.

Decisions Needed Room by Room

Make enough copies of the following checklist so that
you'll have one for each room you plan to remodel.

Flooring Materials

- ☐ Wall-to-wall carpeting
- ☐ Hardwood (strips, parquet)
- ☐ Vinyl (sheet or tiles)
- ☐ Pine planking
- ☐ Ceramic tile
- ☐ Area rugs

Wall Finish and Materials

- ☐ Plaster (smooth or textured)
- ☐ Wallboard and wallpaper
- ☐ Brick or masonry
- ☐ Wood paneling
- ☐ Wallboard and paint
- ☐ Ceramic tile

Wood Trim

- ☐ Baseboards (grade of wood)
- ☐ Door and window trim
- ☐ Finish (paint or stain)
- ☐ Molding (crown, etc.)

Ceiling Materials and Finish

- ☐ Plaster (smooth or textured)
- ☐ Wallboard with paint
- ☐ Exposed beams (real or fake)
- ☐ Drop ceiling
- ☐ Wood paneling, paint, or stain
- ☐ Wallboard with wallpaper
- ☐ Acoustical tile
- ☐ Other

Hardware

- ☐ Window locks
- ☐ Hinges
- ☐ Cabinet and drawer pulls
- ☐ Door knobs and lock sets
- ☐ Coat hooks

Electrical

- ☐ Location of switches (will any control outlets?)
- ☐ Location of outlets
- ☐ Which controlled by switch
- ☐ Location of prewired television cable outlets
- ☐ Location of prewired telephone outlets
- ☐ Light fixtures (recessed, mounted, suspended, spots, floods, table, desk, and floor lamps)
- ☐ Location of prewired electronic equipment (VCR, stereo, speakers, computers, security system)
- ☐ Location of dedicated electrical lines (outlets on a single circuit breaker)
- ☐ Prewired security system

Mechanical

- ☐ Heating method (hookup to central system, auxiliary electric, baseboard electric, space heater, radiant in floor or ceiling, active or passive solar, wood stove, fireplace)
- ☐ Air conditioning (built-in units, window units, central system)
- ☐ Ventilation (exhaust fan, window fan, location of windows)

Decorating

- ☐ Paint color (walls, woodwork, windows, trim, doors)
- ☐ Paint type (oil- or water-based, high-gloss, gloss, flat, matte)
- ☐ Tile pattern (show GC how it should look on floor.)
- ☐ Rug or carpet (pattern, weight, and color)
- ☐ Fabric type and pattern for drapery, furniture, curtains

Windows

- ☐ Match existing
- ☐ Replace or repair
- ☐ Number of panes
- ☐ Separate storms, type of installation
- ☐ Insulated glass
- ☐ Wood, steel, aluminum, vinyl, or metal-clad

CHAPTER 11

The Fine Art of Compromise

(or, Can This Marriage Be Saved?)

Her favorite color is blue, his is brown. He likes country, she prefers modern. She is concerned about costs, he wants only the best. She wants hardwood floors, he wants wall-to-wall carpeting. She wants large expanses of windows, he wants to conserve energy.

When two people come to a remodeling project, they frequently arrive with completely different ideas of what looks good. The ability to compromise is essential, so if you and your spouse haven't worked out a method of dealing with differences up to this point in your relationship, you might as well use your remodeling project as a starting point.

Since Eileen and I were not married when we embarked on our remodel, we were still being polite to each other. We had differences of opinion, but we never got to the point of calling each other names or belittling each other's ideas. People who have been married for years sometimes find this kind of restraint difficult to achieve. Over the years most couples develop shorthand communication techniques. They can almost read each other's minds. Unfortunately, they have also learned what each other's hot buttons are and how to push them. The multitude of decisions that must be made in a remodeling project can put real stress on a relationship. Perhaps the best advice I can give you if you are undertaking a remodeling project with your mate is to resurrect the good behavior that served you so well during your courtship.

Why Remodeling Is
Hard on a Relationship

Your temptation as you read this may be to say, "Pshaw! I have better things to do than to fight nonstop with my husband (or wife)." But take it from those who have been through it before: remodeling is hard on a relationship because . . .

It Totally Disrupts
Your Everyday Routine

Remember how grateful you were to see those weekend houseguests leave, even though they were wonderful? Your remodeling crew is going to be with you five days a week for weeks or even months, and they start by tearing your house apart.

It Involves Family Finances

According to marriage counselors, disagreements involving money outweigh those involving sex as a major cause of stress in a relationship. During a large remodeling project, you're going to have to make hundreds of decisions that involve spending money—more money than you've ever spent since buying your house. And, unless you plan well, more money than you've budgeted.

It Involves Personal Taste

What looks good and what doesn't is a highly subjective matter. Each of us has an innate sense of right and wrong when it comes to design, though in some this sense is more highly developed than in others. If each of you has strong opinions and your opinions are at opposite ends of the taste spectrum, you're in for a rough time. And, unlike deciding what to have for dinner tonight, the remodeling decisions you make are ones you know you're going to have to live with for years to come. No wonder people tend to get uptight.

Design/Builder: *Over 50 percent of the clients we have worked for have ended up divorced. It's a sad statistic and it's one of the big reasons I'm not in the construction business anymore.*

That particular builder was in Vermont where, it seems, metropolitan couples whose marriages are in trouble go to spend more time together and try to heal their union. Of course, the old house they buy needs to be fixed up, but the *togetherness* philosophy doesn't really work when you're covered with plaster dust.

It Spotlights Your Differences

Most relationships succeed by emphasizing the positive. Couples usually know were they disagree and have learned to stay away from those areas, but in a remodel, differences of opinion have to be faced and worked out.

Builder: *A remodeling project will just exacerbate any differences that are already there. If a couple is not able to come up with a compromise solution that they can both live with, it will just fester forever.*

Both of you have to be clear about the rules. One contractor told me about the time he was trying to install fixtures in a small bathroom and the wife kept changing her mind . After the third change he called the husband at work to alert him to the extra charges that were being run up. Within fifteen minutes the husband came screeching into the driveway, ran into the house, sent all the workers outside, and proceeded to chew his wife up one side and down the other. Together they worked out new rules. She was very cooperative for the next few days and stopped making frivolous changes. "That was ten years ago," the contractor observed, "and they're still together."

Homeowner: *I would suggest that any couple contemplating a major remodeling project get in therapy. I'm serious. We did, and I think it saved our marriage.*

It Demands Honesty and Openness

This is not the time to bottle up your opinions and desires because eventually those differences will surface.

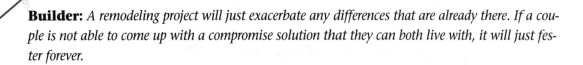

General Contractor: *If they discuss their problems openly in front of you, the job usually goes fine. The situation that causes me the most trouble is where one person, usually the husband, says, "I don't care. You choose what you want." Look out, because what he is saying is, "I don't care until I have to write the check." These are the people who take no part in the decision-making process until the paint is selected and on the wall. Then they say, "Why'd you pick green? You know I can't stand green."*

Another contractor described a situation he had encountered more than once. He called it The Hidden Agenda Syndrome, in which a remodeling project is undertaken to save or delay the end of a marriage: *The wife is delighted at first because she is finally getting her dream, and the husband's attitude is, "Give her anything she wants." That can be the sign of a very generous husband or a man with a guilty conscience who just wants to get his wife off his back. Halfway through the job the wife figures out what's going on and sparks begin to fly.*

There should be a label attached to remodeling plans: "Warning. This project may be hazardous to your marriage."

How Other Remodelers Have Stayed Married

Actually, quite a few of the couples I interviewed for this book stayed married long enough to enjoy their new kitchen or addition. When I asked them how they handled differences of taste and opinion, here's what they said:

"We Resolved Money Questions Right off the Bat."

It seems that most of the problems couples encounter during remodeling can be traced back to the amount of money being spent. The homeowners I interviewed agreed that the best way to handle the money question is to establish a firm budget during the planning phase and agree to stick to it. They also admitted that staying within a budget on every item is like living on a diet. And, as with a diet, if they went over the prescribed allotment in one area, they had to cut back somewhere else.

Homeowner (wife): *Real differences usually came when money was involved. I don't worry about money. I think it will be there if we really need it or if we want something badly enough. But my husband is very concerned with money. I eventually learned to find out how much he had in mind to spend on a particular fixture or appliance before I went out shopping rather than selecting something and then finding out what he had expected to pay.*

Homeowners: *We knew from the beginning we were working on a very tight budget. Since we both were very much aware of costs, if we got into a situation where one of us wanted something that was beyond our means, the other only had to offer a gentle reminder.*

Homeowner (husband): *Yes, we had arguments and differences, and I lost most of them. We have larger windows than I thought we needed, we have a skylight in the bedroom I didn't think we needed. But I must confess I didn't feel strongly about those things, and we were able to find the money. I don't remember our buying anything I really didn't want.*

Homeowner: *We started with a pretty vague plan of what we wanted and a low budget. As the work developed together we realized we were creating some very special space and decided to go with top-of-the-line materials and fixtures. We also went back to the bank for more money.*

"We Resolved Differences of Taste by Being Open-minded."

In many situations the discussion may seem to be about money, but the real difference of opinion is about taste. One couple I questioned had several tactics to solve this problem. This couple has a large, bold, colorful floral pattern fabric on the living-room walls of their small New York apartment. Since the selection of the fabric went considerably beyond which shade of beige would look best, I asked how they had arrived at their choice.

Wife: *This was something I had to convince him of. He thought a big busy pattern would make the room look smaller. I showed him dozens of pictures of teeny English cottages and proved that patterned wallpaper actually makes the rooms look bigger. In fact, the more that is in a room and the busier it is, the better off you are. We had some criteria: It had to have a couple of colors in it, and it had to have some coordinated trim designs that went with it.*

Husband: *She showed me enough pictures of English cottages that I bought the idea, but it took a lot of weekends going blind looking at fabric samples.*

These were two strong-minded people, but neither ran roughshod over the other. Since the husband did much of the remodeling work himself, the wife understood he couldn't very well be expected to work on something unless he agreed that it was a good idea. "I never had to build, move, or tear out something under protest," he said. They both had to agree on something before they started on it.

There is another "taste" problem that came up in one interview but is probably much more widespread than husbands would like to admit.

Wife: *My husband doesn't have any taste. I don't mean he has bad taste. I mean he doesn't have a preference in taste. I think most men relinquish any claim to any decisions in the home very early in a relationship. Very few get into fabric swatches and wallpaper sample books.*

This woman's husband may be like the child who never spoke until one day at the age of eight he said, "This soup needs more salt." When his delighted parents asked why he had never spoken earlier he replied, "Everything's been fine up to now." I suggest that this woman's husband, like many of us, learned that he could rely on her taste and just went along with it.

Another couple had a much easier time of it. Their tastes were similar. They did run into one impasse, however.

Homeowner: *My wife and I have very similar tastes. I tend to be a little bit (actually a lot) more down and dirty, and she likes things more buttoned up. But our basic tastes are alike. One place where we couldn't agree was on the style of a doorknob for the closet just off the kitchen. It's been three years now and it still doesn't have a knob. You need a boyscout knife to get into it.*

"We Broke Impasses by Taking the Time to Work Them Through."

Many of the homeowners I interviewed described a feeling-out process: In the beginning they really didn't know what their opinions were. But as the project began to sort itself out, they were able to lock onto what they wanted. I asked one couple who weathered the process quite well what happened when they locked onto two different things.

Wife: *We hit those situations. I just waited for good opportunities to take up my cause. The power of a drop of water on a stone.*

Husband: *She is patient. Very, very patient. That's the solution, really. You just go away from the problem for a while.*

Wife: *That's really how we solved a problem. We both just stood away from it and let our minds work subconsciously on it, and before long you start incorporating the other person's idea, no matter how resistant you thought you were in the beginning.*

What Happens When You Fail to Communicate?

The previous couples had different views, but they communicated. What happens in the more likely event that one member of the couple is not a great communicator?

> **Wife:** *We made a lot of mistakes. There was a lot of stress involved. I'm married to a guy who doesn't communicate. I remember sitting here one evening speculating about how a set of bookshelves might look on this wall. I think I might even have gone on and on about it. His comment to me was, "We can't afford to do that right now."*
>
> *Then one morning I woke up to the sound of the power saw. I came down and the wall was gone. He was proceeding with the project and asked me if I had any drawings of what I wanted. Unfortunately, he was reacting to what he thought I wanted when in reality I hadn't had time to think it through properly.*

The fascinating thing about this couple is that they worked on the complete renovation of their home for ten years and in that time never quite mastered the art of communicating. They were talking but making assumptions rather than making sure they understood each other.

(Relatively) Painless Ways of Compromising

If you are going to come out of a remodeling project still speaking to each other, you are going to have to find ways to arrive at compromises. You should set up some ground rules before you really need them. Here are some suggestions:

Yield to the Project's Natural Constraints

Fortunately, unless you're blessed with unlimited funds and time, there are certain outside factors that tend to reduce the range of options realistically available to you. This speeds the compromise process and forces your hand.

The budget. The first is the amount of money you have to spend. If the budget is broken down into areas such as electrical fixtures, bathroom fixtures, kitchen appliances, etc., and you agree ahead of time to stay within the budget, it can serve as a check on your decision-making process. Yes, you want to have beautiful things, but they also must be within your budget.

Space. One of you may really want an 8-foot circular bathtub and Jacuzzi combination, but if the whole bathroom is only 5 by 7 it tends to keep the project within the realm of the possible.

Time. You may not believe it, but there is a time limit to your project, and there will be some decisions you'll have to make today because the item in question has to go in tomorrow. If you're in a deadlock in the showroom, you'd better learn how to compromise by closing time.

Make the Best Use of Your Individual Interests and Skills

If you and your spouse got together under the natural rule that says opposites attract, your chances of reaching a compromise may actually be enhanced. If one of you can take charge of the decorating and aesthetic details and the other monitor the mechanical details of construction, you're far less likely to tread on each other's toes.

Architect: *There are some cases where both people are planners or both are detail people, and you have a disaster. The client mix I love the best is where one of them is a planner and likes the feel of the organization of rooms and doesn't care what's on the walls or the floors, and the other is interested in interior decoration. They each get to work at the things that interest them, and they let the other one handle the other stuff.*

Contractor: *The decisions, particularly in the early planning stage, can go a couple of possible ways from my experience: In scenario number one, the wife wants something that is too ambitious, and the husband doesn't want to spend the money. I usually suggest that there is a happy middle ground here where he doesn't have to spend as much as he thinks and she doesn't need quite as big a project as she expects. They have probably been fighting about this for years before I got here. I tell them, "The only reason I'm sitting here is because she's tired of looking at it and he's tired of hearing about it." They laugh and that usually breaks the tension, and we go on from there.*

In the other scenario, one half of the couple is a nitpicker and the other is a fairly reasonable human being. Very seldom do you have a problem with both halves of the couple.

Contractor: *The basic rule of survival for the GC is to "divide and conquer." In most marriages, one partner sits on the money and the other is in charge of wishes and dreams. The GC becomes a marriage counselor, a minister, a financial counselor . . . even a GC at times. He has to walk the thin line between alienating the one who will pay him and the one who will be happy enough with the job to say, "Pay him."*

Take the Time to Settle on a Style for Your Home

Do you want country, Shaker, Southwestern, modern, English cottage, Arts & Crafts, Victorian? To help you decide, go back to your file of magazine pictures and peruse them together, pointing out room arrangements and decorating touches that you like. Once you land on a style you both like, you'll have effectively limited your selections to a manageable number of items consistent with the style you've chosen.

Of course, if you can't agree on an overall style, there is no law that says you can't mix two or three of them. It might be best not to mix styles in any single room, but if one of you has his or her heart set on a frilly Victorian look, designate one of the guest rooms for this treatment. I call this approach "divide and concur."

Here's how it worked in my house. I happen to like dark forest-green walls. My wife wanted bone white. Any compromise between those two colors would have looked like a mental hospital, and neither of us would have been happy. So, I have dark green walls in my office and the rest of the house is bone white.

We had a terrible time picking the tiles for the floors and showers in the two bathrooms. It was pretty obvious we had two different decorative schemes in mind, so we split up the task. I got to do the upstairs bathroom and she did the downstairs bathroom. I suspect she was looking over my shoulder as I made my selections, but that's *my* tan tile and desert sage linoleum in there.

Treat Remodeling Decisions like Business Decisions

Think hard about how you arrive at decisions and compromises at work and use the same techniques with your spouse. Don't whine or sulk, or rant and rave; instead, treat each other as business partners in this venture. Ask and question. Don't demand. Suggest alternatives. Ask for time to think about your partner's suggestions, and if you reach impasses, you might take a leaf from basketball's held-ball rule and take turns making the final decision. Just make sure you keep track of whose turn it is.

Architect: *I've seen it work where both people are management types and they handle their discussions like an office situation. They treat it like professionals. They use the same type of etiquette: "What do you think?" or "Well, how about this approach?" More or less impersonal and polite. These are the couples who tend to work out the decisions.*

CHAPTER
12

What to Do
When Things Go Wrong
(and They Will)

The purpose of this book is to help you plan your remodeling project so thoroughly that you'll have anticipated every contingency and avoided every mistake. Hah—fat chance. I'm reminded of the contractor who told us that every time he bid a job he assumed it was going to be the first perfect job in recorded history. You're likely to be optimistic at the outset—and disappointed, to some degree or another, later on. The reality of the situation is that despite your best efforts, I'm afraid there *will* be mistakes on your job.

It's not so much what goes wrong but how you and your contractor react to it that will determine how destructive and disruptive the mistakes on your job become. One of the architects I talked to presented an interesting approach to eliminating a lot of mistakes—he simply called them "a matter of perception."

Architect: *I'm not sure what a "mistake" is in construction. Often homeowners approve ideas, sketches, and plans all along and never admit that they can't read drawings. The first time they see their house in three dimensions is during the framing stage and they say, "That's not what we thought it would look like. Can we change it?"*

That's not a mistake. That's a matter of perception. We have found that most cost overruns occur because the owners make changes as they see their dream coming true and say, "You know, I wouldn't mind spending a little more if we could change that."

Types of Mistakes
and How to Handle Them

Mistakes come in many forms. There are those of omission, where something that should have been done wasn't done, and those of commission, where something that should not have been done was done or done incorrectly. Then there are those where something is done correctly according to the plans, but it just doesn't look right.

The most common reasons mistakes happen include the following:

Lack of Planning

If a remodeling project is progressing without working drawings, mistakes will be made because problems can't be foreseen. Mistakes come from not looking three steps ahead and anticipating problems. You find out the Jacuzzi won't fit through the new bathroom door, tear out the wall, then discover the Jacuzzi could have been taken apart. That's a mistake—or two.

Different Points of View

Sometimes a mistake, like beauty, is in the eye of the beholder. Our last-minute "divided pane" picture-window project comes to mind. The contractor and I thought the wooden snap-in grids looked just fine. To my wife the fake grids were a mistake. Fortunately it was a mistake that only cost $25 to make, and, if it had worked, we would have saved about $1,200, but it would have bothered my wife forever after.

Well-intentioned Mistakes

There is a law in physics that says for every action there is an equal and opposite reaction. That seems to hold true for good intentions in construction. The lead carpenter on our project wanted to make sure I had enough headroom in the upstairs shower, which is built under the eaves. So in laying out the roof rafters, he raised the peak some 4 extra feet. To my wife this made the house look like a tepee. To her eyes, the roof was completely out of scale.

This change was made one morning when the roof rafters went up. We didn't get a vote. We could have insisted on a fix, but it would have cost a lot of extra money, and we weren't sure the roof would really look out of proportion when it was finished. (My wife still thinks the roof looks completely out of scale, even after years of my driving around pointing out steep-roofed houses.)

I did get to vote on another change in that bathroom. The original chimney, which was tucked away in the attic crawl space of the ranch, was now the inside wall of the second-floor bathroom. No one had noticed, but the chimney canted about a foot and a half toward the front of the house and into the bathroom before it headed toward the roof. When I visited the site one morning, I asked the carpenter why he had a two-by-four propped against the chimney. He removed the prop, grabbed the chimney with both hands, and made it sway about 6-inches back and forth. "That's why," he said.

He suggested tearing out the old bent chimney and putting in a new cinder-block chimney that would go straight up. He explained that we could even salvage the used bricks and use them for the part that would show above the roof. It was a great idea and I went along with it immediately. The rearranged chimney added a foot and a half to the width of the bathroom, which meant that we hadn't needed to raise the peak of the roof to get my headroom in the shower after all.

Was raising the roof a mistake? It was a good decision at the time because it gave me headroom. My wife tends to believe that if we had retained an architect, he or she would have crawled around in the attic, made accurate measurements, and solved the problem on paper before we discovered it in real life. Maybe.

Underbids by Contractors or Subcontractors

This starts out being the contractor's mistake and the contractor's problem, but you end up becoming involved. If the contractor has uncovered some previously unanticipated problems like rotten floor joists under the bathtub or piping that has to be replaced, he has a right to get additional money for additional work, and the contract probably provides for this, even if it is a firm-bid contract (see chapter 4).

If, however, you suspect your contractor gave you an artificially low bid just to get the job and is now trying to stick it to you, you have an obligation to your fellow homeowners to give him a very hard time. Don't do what this couple did.

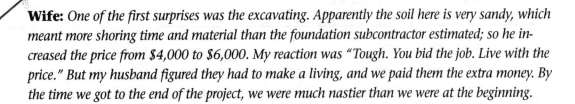

Wife: *One of the first surprises was the excavating. Apparently the soil here is very sandy, which meant more shoring time and material than the foundation subcontractor estimated; so he increased the price from $4,000 to $6,000. My reaction was "Tough. You bid the job. Live with the price." But my husband figured they had to make a living, and we paid them the extra money. By the time we got to the end of the project, we were much nastier than we were at the beginning.*

Lack of Necessary Skills

Sometimes a contractor will take on a task that is beyond his experience and abilities. This is how one homeowner handled the situation with a minimum of discomfort.

Homeowner: *Departing from our do-it-yourself policy last spring, I ran into a contractor I knew and asked if he did screened-in porches. He said he did, came around to see the porch, and made an estimate of $1,200 including materials—tops $1,500.*

He came and started doing the work. At the end of the week he said, "Where's my money?" So I gave him $300 on top of the $400 I had already paid him to cover the materials. It was obvious he had never done a screened porch before. When he got to the last $300 or $400, he wanted me to pay him. I pointed out he hadn't finished. He said, "You pay me and I'll finish." and I said, "No. You finish and I'll pay you." He never came back.

I think what happened was the job ended up being more difficult than he thought, and when he pulled off it was at the break-even point. If he finished the job he was going to lose money, and even if I had paid him I doubt if he would have been back.

Wrong Deliveries

Even with all the electronic order-processing gear in use today, or maybe because of it, a lot of the things that arrive at your house will not be what you ordered. When this happens you have two clear choices: keep it or send it back.

If you're reading this before you remodel, you may feel the obvious answer is to send it back. But once you're in the midst of a remodel, you'll understand that timing is a consideration. When we discovered the lumberyard had sent us the wrong-color roofing shingles, they were in a pile in the backyard. We sent them back. But what if the crew had already covered half the roof with the wrong shingles? Who would have paid for the extra labor of redoing the whole job? Who, in fact, made the mistake? The contractor? The supplier? Or had I been unclear about the color? Fortunately, we never had to find out.

You may find yourself in a similar situation. You can see the time clock running as the debate goes on, and you know that the weather report calls for heavy rain tomorrow. Suddenly the new color doesn't look so bad after all.

Homeowner: *I had ordered kitchen cabinets with polished-brass pulls and blind hinges. What came in was antique brass face-mounted "H" hinges with polished-brass knobs that didn't match. It was the fault of the guy who took my order. He wrote down blind hinges, but manufacturers just look at style numbers on the order form, and this guy had written down the wrong numbers. We had waited fifteen weeks and had planned a party to show off our new kitchen. We were running behind so I had two choices: We could accept them as they were and have polished-brass hinges put on to match the pulls or we could send them back and wait another sixteen to eighteen weeks. We kept them. Some of those things you have to just accept. But I'm still not happy about them.*

Judgment Calls

The original oak flooring in our living room and front bedroom runs north and south. The oak flooring in the big new room across the back of the house runs east and west. Right up until I was writing this paragraph, I thought it was because the floor joists under the new section went in a different direction from those under the rest of the house. I just went downstairs and looked. They run from north to south just like the front rooms' joists.

Is it a mistake to have the flooring running the entire length of a room rather than across it to match the rest of the house? It probably wasn't a mistake as much as it was a surprise. I just assumed it would run the other way. I certainly didn't feel strongly enough about it to have the new floor ripped up and relaid.

As you will undoubtedly discover, it seems you only get to discuss these problems after the work is done. A seam runs right down the middle of the kitchen countertop or your deck is a different shape than you thought it would be. Are these mistakes? Should they be done over? It depends on how tired of remodeling you are.

It's Done Right but It Looks Wrong

You agreed to the plans, you watched it being built, and now you don't like the way it looks. It could be the location of the front stairs or a kitchen window, the size of the master bedroom, the color of your living-room walls, or the location of the built-in dinette. This happens a lot, so don't feel bad. The trick is to discover these "mistakes" as early as possible in the building process. It is easier and less expensive to move a stud wall than a wall that has been completely finished. So speak up as soon as you notice something.

You are the ones who are going to have to live with your remodel. If you aren't happy with it now, it's probably not going to get better with time. Stop the work and talk to your GC. Tell him how you feel and what you'd like. He may have some suggestions that will solve your problem. If not, he can tell you how much it will cost to tear out what has been done and rebuild it to your satisfaction.

Builder: *People will get over the price of something a lot quicker than they will it being wrong. The extra $200 or $2,000 is not going to be as big an issue ten years from now as the light switch you can't reach from your bed. Every single night it is going to bother you. . . . Every night.*

In our case there was one thing we felt strongly enough about to change—the closet doors in the master bedroom. For some reason the swing direction of these doors has been a major point of debate from the first moment we put them on paper right up to the present.

The thing we learned is that a closet may seem large in the plans, but when you have clothes poles on three sides and the door opens into the closet, you can barely turn around, and half the clothes are blocked by the door. We both opted to have the doors changed to swing out. Mine works fine but Eileen's now tangles with the bedroom door.

How to Handle Mistakes

Everyone I talked to—architects, home builders, and homeowners—reported that mistakes were made on every job they had ever been involved with. There are going to be mistakes made on your job too. Your first inclination may be to scream and point fingers, but that is not the best way to reach a solution to a problem. Here is a better step-by-step approach:

Check the Agreement

What do the specifications call for? (This is why you want a fairly detailed agreement or contract.) If the bid called for ten electrical outlets and there are only eight, your problem is fairly easy to resolve. Ask your contractor to put in two more outlets. If there are ten and you want more, be prepared to spend an additional twenty-five dollars apiece.

Keep Good Records

Like a spicy meatball dinner, mistakes will return to give you more discomfort unless you keep thorough records of what was wrong, what action was agreed upon, what additional costs were agreed to, and what settlement or compromise (if any) you and the builder or supplier agreed to. If you don't keep records, you will have to relive the entire episode when it comes time to settle up and everyone has forgotten what they said or agreed to.

The key is to document all such transactions with *change orders*. A change order is like a small contract negotiated in the midst of a project that adds, subtracts, or changes materials or labor on a job. Your contractor should have a change-order form for both of you to sign. Additional costs from changes are one of the biggest causes of disputes between builders and homeowners when it comes time to settle up.

Find out Why It Was Done This Way

Try to make your first reaction to an apparent mistake curiosity rather than anger. Every construction job is a learning experience for everyone concerned: the crew, the contractor, and certainly the homeowners.

Builder: *Before you blow up, find out why something was done the way it was. There may be a very sound, structural reason why it had to be done that way. Your GC should be willing to give you that explanation. If he has done something that you really want different, and it isn't against any basic law of nature (like gravity), make your feelings very clear before he goes any further.*

Sometimes even being very clear isn't enough. I wanted a laundry chute. I drew it into the plans for the upstairs bathroom. I had it coming down through the hall closet. Unfortunately, it had to drop all the clothes behind the furnace, but I thought we could work that out. I hung on to that laundry chute through every revision of the plans. I finally lost it when my GC showed me I was 3 feet off in my calculations between the two floors. I briefly entertained bringing it down through the bookcase in the living room, but a cooler head prevailed. There comes a time when pet projects must be abandoned.

Stay Calm and Talk with Your GC

Contractor: *Hopefully you haven't stopped communicating, so when something goes wrong you can figure out how to solve it. If the two parties are mad at each other or don't respect each other, there is no way they are going to be able to talk about what went wrong.*

Try to determine how the mistake at hand happened and who was responsible for it. Often you'll find everyone has contributed a little to the problem by making assumptions rather than communicating clearly. This is the time to find out what it will cost to correct the mistake and how that cost will be allocated.

Step Back and Look at It

Ask yourself, "Is this really wrong? Does this look awful, or could we live with it?" Like the direction of our oak flooring, some things aren't mistakes, they are surprises. A good policy is to go away and sleep on it before you make a final decision. Is this something neither one of you feels particularly strongly about? If so, maybe you should adapt.

Tear It out and Do It Over

If whatever has happened is wrong or could be better and it really bothers you, bite the bullet and have the contractor tear it out. It's your house, and as long as you're willing to pay for it, it should look the way you want it to be. But try to be decisive. Adding several days of indecision to an awkward situation just runs up the cost and frustration.

Do try to remember that your carpenter or builder has spent time, effort, and possibly some loving creativity building the thing you are asking him to tear out, so be diplomatic and considerate in the way you approach the subject.

Builder: *I've told my present client, "One of the things I really dislike is tearing up my work and doing it again." And it isn't even the money, because I'm going to get paid to tear it up and to redo it. It's a human thing. I know I'm going to make mistakes and the client is going to make mistakes, but it doesn't make it any easier.*

Send It Back

If the problem is with some product or material that has been delivered from the lumberyard, let your GC know you are unhappy and then let *him* deal with it.

Contractor: *The contractor is in a better position to negotiate with a lumberyard or supplier because he is buying $200,000 worth of materials a year.*

If you're like I am, you hate to bother people by complaining, and you hate to send things back. I once kept shoes from a mail-order house that didn't quite fit rather than send them back. Fortunately, I got over that phase and have discovered that the mail-order people don't think any less of you if you return something. You don't even have to tell them why.

The point of this little digression is to impress upon you that you have the right to have the correct product delivered. Like mail-order houses, lumberyards, showrooms, and even manufacturers are used to having people return things, even when they have delivered the right item, so your effort to return something that is wrong should meet little resistance. You will still be considered a nice person.

Accept It but Negotiate

It's wrong, but it's already installed and it took six months to deliver. You have decided that removing the item would be a major hassle. The question you have to ask your GC and, in turn, the supplier of the wrong material is, Should you pay full price? Your poker-playing skills may come in handy here. You are going to have to convince the supplier that he or she can come and take back the product and that you are willing to wait for the right product to be delivered. When suppliers calculate the cost of transportation, the time of their people, and their chances of selling the returned item to someone else, they may offer you a substantial discount or some additional service . . . and you deserve it.

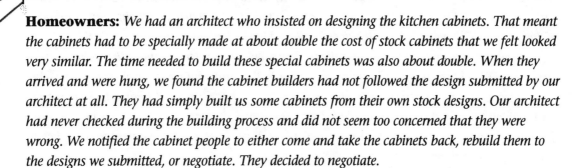

Homeowners: *We had an architect who insisted on designing the kitchen cabinets. That meant the cabinets had to be specially made at about double the cost of stock cabinets that we felt looked very similar. The time needed to build these special cabinets was also about double. When they arrived and were hung, we found the cabinet builders had not followed the design submitted by our architect at all. They had simply built us some cabinets from their own stock designs. Our architect had never checked during the building process and did not seem too concerned that they were wrong. We notified the cabinet people to either come and take the cabinets back, rebuild them to the designs we submitted, or negotiate. They decided to negotiate.*

We are now living with cabinets we don't really like, but we have a large serving island that we did not have to pay for. It is not placed correctly in the room (the back door hits it, and it is too far from the kitchen countertops), but saving some money helped.

Preventive Medicine

The best way to handle mistakes is to prevent them, and the best way to prevent them is to plan thoroughly before you start and think three steps ahead. If you and your contractor are looking ahead, you have a better chance of catching mistakes early or even before they happen. But the most important way to keep mistakes from becoming disasters is to keep the lines of communications open. Let your GC know if you feel something looks wrong.

Design/Remodeler: *We have found if you talk to your clients once in a while before something goes wrong, communication is better. We try to ask our clients at least once a week, "How are things?" And we don't mean the weather. We want to know if anything is bothering them, and more often than not they will tell us all the good things that have happened.*

If you ask them about it, they're usually happy. But if they have to call you up and tell you about a mistake, the phone may explode in your hands. I guess the rule is: If you're able to talk about it, you can solve it.

Another way to prevent mistakes is to check out the work each day and find out from your contractor when a major step in the construction process is going to take place. The homeowners who took off for California for two months found a lot of problems when they got back.

Homeowner: *The contractor we selected, who seemed to be fairly reliable, was sick for a good part of the job, and his crew who did the work weren't as skillful. There is a slight ramp into each of the upstairs bathrooms because the floors in the addition don't meet the original floors.*

While we were away someone installed a very peculiar banister. We made them change the angle and design of the banister, but the pocket door to the bathroom never has worked right since the painter tried to remove the slide mechanism with a crowbar. Our grandchildren tacked up a DUCK *sign on the new stairs to protect the unwary from the low overhead that was created because the builder apparently felt a flat floor in an upstairs storage closet was more important than head-room on the front stairs.*

The house looks great and the view of the harbor through the new picture windows is spectacular. Only the owner and his wife know where all the mistakes are. He knows his builder has gotten additional jobs from people who have seen their remodeled home, but not one has asked him if he would recommend the builder. If you want an accurate assessment of a contractor, you must talk to the homeowners when you check out his references.

And Now, a Golden Opportunity to Learn from *Our* Experience (or The Case of the Casement Windows)

If you are going to approach your first remodeling project as though it were your second, as we promised, here's a chance to learn from our mistakes. Eileen and I knew we wanted our windows divided into small panes of glass. But we also wanted some increased insulation value over a single layer of glass. When we toured the building-supply company, we learned that it was possible to have small-pane thermopane windows with wide mullions (the wood between the panes), although they would be very expensive. We didn't like the look of the wide mullions, and we didn't like the idea of paying extra for something we didn't like the look of. So we opted for single-layer glass, narrow mullions and a form of storm window called *button-on*. There were five people involved in this decision and in taking the order: my wife and me, our builder, my brother, who once represented a window manufacturer and understood all the terms, and the building-supply salesman. It was not a hasty process.

We didn't see the windows until six weeks later, after they were all in place . . . and wrong. They had the single sheet of glass, but they also had the wide wooden mullions that we went to so much trouble to avoid. These windows were a major part of the family room (or sun room—we never have hit on a name for it). The wooden dividers looked huge as we stood and stared at them. We went home and came back the next morning, and they didn't look so bad. It was also February in Connecticut. The windows were needed. Finally, we reluctantly accepted them.

A week later the builder called to say that the French-door unit for that same family room was in. This was a three-piece unit of floor-to-ceiling windows with a swing door onto the deck. As we drove over I asked Eileen if she was preparing herself mentally for the windows in this unit to be "right." "Oh Lord," was all she said. And right they were. The window manufacturer had been able to provide French doors with narrow-mullioned small-paned windows. The unit occupied one-third of the wall space and was between the other windows. Now we stood and stared at the variety of windows. "Can we live with it?" we asked ourselves. Again, we decided we could.

The truth of the matter is, no one notices the variety of windows. They all really do look fine, which speaks well for the mistake-handling technique called adapting. But what if they *hadn't* looked right? How should we have handled the problem then?

What We Should Have Done

Since our little episode with the windows, I've learned that we should have lodged a complaint, through our contractor, with the building-supply house. With our four witnesses in tow, we should have met with the window salesman and his manager and checked the order that they sent out to the window manufacturer. Either the order was right and the manufacturer built it wrong, the order was wrong when it went to the manufacturer, or we ordered the wrong windows. We knew right off the bat that the latter was unlikely.

If the manufacturer had made the mistake, we could have retained the original windows until the manufacturer supplied the correct ones and then possibly negotiated an allowance to cover the contractor's time for replacement.

If the salesman had made the mistake, it would have been up to him to work out something with the manufacturer to replace the windows. Failing that, he should have offered us some discount. The building-supply house should not have been paid in full for a mistake, and we should not have been asked to pay full price for the wrong product.

Of course, the moral of this story is that a supplier doesn't have much of a chance to correct a mistake if you don't let him know about it. I suspect our contractor should have known about these options and pressed our case, but we aren't really unhappy with the results.

Insurance:
When Things Go Wrong,
Are You Covered?

I alerted you in chapter 2 to the hazards of hiring contractors who are not insured (you could be held liable). One of the couples I interviewed offered an example of the kind of disaster that can happen. Their story illustrates the perils you can encounter during a remodel. Be sure to check out your contractor's coverage.

Homeowner: *While moving the electrical lines on the house, the contractor let them sag too low over the highway in front of the house, and just at that moment a motorcycle went by. The guy hit the wire, just like in the movies.*

It made us realize that one question we hadn't asked at the beginning of all this was whether our contractor was insured and bonded. In that particular part of Pennsylvania, anyone with a set of tools and a pickup truck could call themselves a contractor without adding all those expensive things like insurance. Fortunately, our contractor was insured and the bike rider was not badly hurt, but he did put in a small claim and the insurance company paid off.

We did learn from this experience, so when we remodeled our New York apartment, we took out an umbrella liability policy over our homeowners' policy because we felt a contractor could show us he had insurance today but he might not have it tomorrow.

Basic Mistakes
Made by Consumers

There are times in remodeling and construction when problems go beyond honest mistakes and misunderstandings and approach the area of fraud. A door-to-door salesman offers to re-side a house and gets the owner to pay the full price up front before he starts, then disappears with the money. Or a homeowner will accept a very low bid on a job and wind up paying several times the contracted price in the end.

It is usually futile to expect to get your money back or the job done correctly, but homeowners, by registering their complaints with the Better Business Bureau or their state's consumer protection agency can help alert others to such scams.

The most frequently mentioned mistakes that homeowners admit to when reporting a problem to the consumer-protection people are:

- We took the first bid.
- We took the lowest bid.
- We didn't get a written contract.
- We gave the contractor all the money up front.
- We hired a contractor with a crew from out of state who offered a much lower price, took the money, did a terrible job, and disappeared.

If you follow the advice I have offered for selecting a contractor (see chapter 2), you should be able to avoid being defrauded, but you will probably not be able to avoid all mistakes and misunderstandings. They are part of the remodeling process. How well you handle them and how objective you are will determine the climate you and your contractor will be working in for the remainder of your project. Look for solutions together—*don't* become part of the problem.

CHAPTER
13

Are You
Part of the Problem?

There are bad builders in the world. There are also difficult and unreasonable clients. It would be poetic justice if they always got together on the same projects, but it doesn't happen that way. You probably don't see yourself as a difficult personality, but every contractor I interviewed had a story about a client from hell. In this chapter I'll give you a list of "don'ts" and a few "dos" that will smooth your relationship with your builder, his crew, and the subcontractors as they work on your project.

How We Kept the Peace
with Our Builder

We started dealing with our builder in October when we selected him from the three we interviewed. The job was finished in June, and the last official thing he did on the house was replace a frozen outdoor faucet the following spring. The fact that he came back to fix something he had no obligation to fix shows we were probably okay to work for.

We Didn't Try to Live in the Job Site

Eileen and I took up residence in my apartment, a couple of towns away, because it's easier to be nice to your builder when you are not living on the premises as he rips them apart.

All the same, I visited the site just about every day. As the days got longer, both of us often came back after Eileen got home from work. Most of the time we just admired the builder's progress, but if we had any questions or found something wrong, I would talk to the builder in person the next day.

We Tried Not to Overreact

I have a sense of humor that I usually manage to maintain in even the most trying situations, but I remember a few scenes that bordered on the tragic. We started the job in January. The builder's first task was to gut the three rooms at the back of the house. Because the power was off, there was no heat. When I arrived late one morning the crew, using a portable generator, was cutting up our ceiling joists and wall studs and burning them in the living-room fireplace to keep from freezing. Now *that* was startling.

I was again impressed the day I stood in what used to be our kitchen with an unobstructed view of the sky and watched the crew take a chain saw to the entire back wall of the house and drop it across the new extended foundation. "I thought you guys were suppose to be *builders*," I said, as I stood among the meager remains of our house.

We Suggested Revisions, but Quietly

I tried to behave myself during our remodeling project, which meant I made the selections I had to make on time, closed my eyes to the hundreds of white plastic coffee cups littering every available surface, and didn't demand that the crew turn down their portable radio. I think the worst thing I did to my builder and his lead carpenter was to show up with a revised set of plans every week or so. In my own defense, I was not asking for drastic changes. One set of plans called for a few changes of door-swing directions, another moved some of the wall plugs and switches around, and one memorable plan quadrupled the number of telephone outlets. (They actually did that one.)

The builder and his crew referred to these revisions as Duncan's-plan-of-the-week, and I inevitably found them a couple of days later under a pile of sawdust with footprints all over them. Our builder didn't actually throw them away; he just didn't pay much attention to them. When it came time to hang the doors and mark the locations for plugs and switches, however, he did come to me and ask where I wanted them. Since I had gone through the exercise of drawing new plans, I knew.

We Didn't Complain

I am fairly easygoing by nature, but I may have been a little too laid back in a couple of instances. For example, I should have objected more strenuously when the windows came in with the wrong mullions and used the negotiating weight of my builder to get the manufacturer or lumberyard to make adjustments (see chapter 12). But for every time I thought I might have lost a little by being too agreeable, such as accepting the different tile pattern on the floor of the downstairs bath or letting one of the crew sleep in the house, there were other instances where I think I gained. They put in a built-in bookcase in the bedroom for free and switched the swing direction on both closet doors at our request . . . twice.

How to Avoid Being
Part of the Problem

If there's a moral to this story, it's that getting along with and cooperating with your builder yields much better results than confrontation and threats. You should view the rest of this chapter as a short charm-school course in how to get on your builder's good side.

Don't Put Your Convenience Ahead of Your Builder's

According to the builders I talked to, an amazing number of homeowners can't adjust to having a building crew in their home. They try to carry on life as usual.

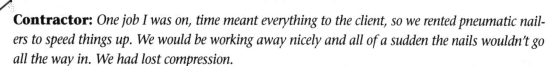

Contractor: *One job I was on, time meant everything to the client, so we rented pneumatic nailers to speed things up. We would be working away nicely and all of a sudden the nails wouldn't go all the way in. We had lost compression.*

It seemed the wife had washing she felt had to be dried that day, so she kept unplugging our compressor and plugging in her drier. I would go downstairs and unplug the drier and plug in our compressor. After four trips to the basement, we went back to swinging hammers. She couldn't grasp the concept that a compressor doesn't have to be "running" all the time to be on. That night I had to explain to the husband why we were hand-nailing and why the job was going to take an extra week. Her explanation was that the children needed clean clothes and she only unplugged the compressor when it wasn't running.

Don't Squander Your Financial Resources

It may be in your bank account, but that's not really your money. It has been committed to your remodeling project, and you will owe it to your contractor.

Contractor: *A new car shows up in the driveway while you're building an addition. Where did it come from? It came out of the house budget. And then you hear, "We're out of money and we can't pay for the windows."*

The bank's approval of a major remodeling project for financing will put more actual cash in your bank account than you may have ever seen there at one time. This is a heady experience. There are those who don't handle it well. Some of the builders I talked to suggested putting the money in a joint escrow account at the bank, which requires the signature of both the homeowner and the contractor to withdraw funds.

Don't Expect to Use Your Contractor's Discounts

Many homeowners are intrigued by the contractor's discount at the building-supply store and begin to think they have some right to it. Businesslike contractors will say "No" because all of them have had an unhappy experience like this:

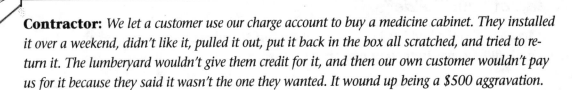

Contractor: *We let a customer use our charge account to buy a medicine cabinet. They installed it over a weekend, didn't like it, pulled it out, put it back in the box all scratched, and tried to return it. The lumberyard wouldn't give them credit for it, and then our own customer wouldn't pay us for it because they said it wasn't the one they wanted. It wound up being a $500 aggravation.*

Don't Expect Your Builder to Be as Neat as Your Mother

If you're a neat freak by nature, try to suspend the urge during a remodeling project. If you don't, you are going to be unhappy. Let the crew make as much mess during working hours as they need. Most contracts call for the job site to be "broom clean" at the end of each day. That gets the major lumps out of your way, but it also raises a final cloud of dust to mark their departure.

Contractor: *Before you start a job, it's a good idea to walk around the house. If you see that the garage floor is painted and the basement floor is painted and waxed and there are plastic covers over the furniture in the living room, it might be best to pass up the job. Dust is going to drive these people crazy. Driving on the lawn for deliveries, parking in their driveway, is going to be a violation of their home. Everyone is going to be unhappy on this job.*

During a remodel is a good time to take advantage of all those lunch and dinner invitations you've been saving up for the past year. A good technique is to invite your neighbors, friends, and family to tour the project after working hours. This will get them involved and alert them to your plight; ideally, it will also result in more invitations to visit, eat out, and let your kids sleep over.

Don't Leave Nasty Notes for Your Contractor to Find

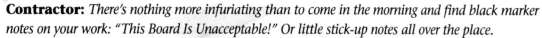

Contractor: *There's nothing more infuriating than to come in the morning and find black marker notes on your work: "This Board Is Unacceptable!" Or little stick-up notes all over the place.*

I did a cedar-shingled "roof" inside a kitchen on the exhaust-fan area. There were about six shingles that were a little lighter than the rest. When I came in the next morning, there were big black X's on them. I felt like taking an ax to the whole thing.

As we saw in chapter 9, communication with your contractor can be a problem if you get home after she has left and you're gone before she gets to your place in the morning; so you leave a note. You think you're leaving a gentle reminder. She thinks you're screaming at her.

Make every effort to set up times when you and your contractor can meet face to face. Join the crew for lunch occasionally, meet before work begins, after hours, in the evening, or weekends. If you're not talking regularly, you're going to be in trouble.

Don't Pull the "Oh, While You're Here" Ploy

Just because you finally have someone in your house who can actually fix a leaky faucet, patch a hole in the plaster, or build a set of bookshelves, you do not automatically get to use those skills for your pet projects. Those little jobs represent additional time that your contractor has not calculated into the price for your project. If you aren't charged for them, the contractor is cheating himself.

If you have some tasks you would like the crew to work on, ask for an estimate and treat each one as separate project. Let them decide if they have the time to spare and want to do the jobs.

Architect: *I had a client who decided he wanted a built-in bookcase in his living room after we had a remodeling project going on in his house. He came to me for the design, and then we offered the job to the GC and also to an outside carpenter I knew for a bid. The carpenter came in with the better bid and we went with him. Since we had discussed this with the GC ahead of time and given him a chance to bid, there was no problem having another carpenter on the premises.*

Don't Use Your Professional Skills to Beat Up on Your Builder

I asked the contractors I interviewed if there were any types of homeowners or particular professions that they avoided like the plague. There are a few—but for a variety of reasons.

> **Contractor:** *Engineers are difficult because they are looking for quality and tolerances that simply do not exist in home construction with its use of wood.*

The legal profession seems to hold a special place in the hearts of the building trades, the most common complaint being about lawyers refusing to pay their bills and telling the builder to take them to court. One such story came up at a home-builders symposium. A building firm had completed a $15,000 remodeling job for a lawyer client who admitted the job had been done perfectly. "So, sue me," he told them when he refused to pay.

> **Contractor:** *I won't do any job for a lawyer unless it is a personal friend, because when I was just starting in the business, I laid out a brick sidewalk for a lawyer. The plans called for it to be 24 inches wide and it wound up 23½ inches. He berated me about how he would have to tear it all up and do over because it was wrong. I was young and more easily intimidated then. He never paid me and the walk has been there since 1972. He used a technicality to beat me out of my pay.*

Several contractors felt that accountants or anyone who works with numbers were likely to be difficult, but one designer said he tries to put the professional skills of such clients to good use.

> **Designer:** *If you can use the skills of your client to help save them money, all the better. Let the CPA help you keep track of the invoices and billing. You are going to be up to your hips in contracts; if the guy's a lawyer, let him take care of them. Give him the sample contract out of the AIA book.*

Don't Try to Supply All the Materials for the Job

When I heard this complaint, I realized it was one I was guilty of. I now suggest you let the builder have a 10 percent commission on the materials he buys for your job because that at least covers his overhead. Renovations and remodeling jobs are not usually heavy users of materials, but you can put your GC's schedule out of whack by not getting the basic supplies to him on time or ordering the wrong things. Let your GC take care of it.

Don't Change Your Mind
from Day to Day

Indecision is the biggest complaint builders have against homeowners. When you can't come to a decision about the location of the door into your bedroom or the fixtures for the bathroom, it can cause delays. When you change your mind after the door has gone in and you force your builder to tear it out and do it over again, you cause his blood pressure to sky-rocket. In either case the cost of the project is increased.

Do Keep Accurate Records
of the Changes You Order

For your sanity and that of your builder, insist that clear, detailed records of changes are kept. (See the section on change orders in chapter 4.) They are the best defense against those last-minute arguments over the bill that destroy what may have been a pleasant business relationship.

Do Treat Your Contractor the Way
You Would Like to Be Treated

I once worked for a manager in a recreation area in Vermont who was convinced that every tradesperson and contractor was out to cheat him and the company. He had his attorney write excruciatingly detailed contracts to protect himself from "these local robbers." The tradespeople took great delight in following the exact letter of those contracts. They charged him for every mile driven, accounted for every minute, and when he made changes during a project (which he invariably did), they hit him with huge cost-plus charges. He expected to get cheated and he was.

I work under the assumption that people are honest and will try to help. I find they usually are and do.

Do Be Willing to Compromise

If you followed the suggestions on how to select a contractor in chapter 2, you should be dealing with an honest, capable building professional. That's a good start. You'll still run into mistakes and misunderstandings, but deal with each other with mutual respect rather than as adversaries. Be open to discussion, be reasonable, and listen. Try to find out what went wrong and why. Then work out a compromise that hurts each of you a little. (That's a sign of a good settlement.)

If you have hired an honest builder, she has a right to expect to be dealing with an honest client. Besides, unless you are a lawyer, going to court is an unsatisfactory, expensive way to settle problems, and both parties usually wind up losing.

Do Keep the Kids out of the Way

No matter how many kids the carpenter may have at home, or how wonderfully the crew gets along with your toddlers, children should not be allowed into the work area during working hours, as we saw in chapter 8. There are simply too many things that can happen and they are all bad.

Do Pay Your Bills on Time

Pay your bills when they are presented in accordance with the bill-paying procedure outlined in your contract. Don't make your builder hound you or beg to get paid.

Don't Beat Your GC to Death for the Final 10 Percent He's Due

As I'll discuss in the next chapter, the final payment on a construction or remodeling contract usually contains most of the profit your builder will make on your job. Don't keep him waiting for it until every last-minute detail meets with your approval. You don't hold back 10 percent of the cost of your steak from the butcher until after the barbecue. Why make it so tough for your GC?

Remember: Your contractor's future business depends on keeping you happy with his work. So you are not entirely dependent on that last 10 percent of the payment to get satisfaction.

CHAPTER
14

Wrapping Up

You may think your remodeling project will never be finished. After the fast start—the demolition and the rough construction—the work has settled into a regular if disruptive routine that shows some progress every day. You've learned to live with the noise, the dust, and the picnics in the living room. You've made a hobby of visiting showrooms. You've made countless decisions. At this point you feel a certain pride in the fact that you've personally selected every tile and knob, every hinge and faucet, every nail and board that has gone into your home. But you're getting very tired of devoting your whole life to the project.

Toward the end, when the finish carpenter and the painters take over, it's harder to see any daily progress because the work is more detailed and seems to stay in the same room day after day. Your patience and your bank account are running out at the same rate. But hang in there: It's almost over. There are only a few last-minute details you have to take care of to ensure that you get the best job possible and to protect your investment. Here are some of them.

The Punch List

A *punch list* is a list of all the little things you notice that haven't been done, have been done incorrectly, are missing parts or pieces, or don't work right. One contractor I interviewed said he was sure it's called a punch list because everyone concerned with the job is so frustrated they're ready to punch each other out.

The punch list is sort of a litmus test for the whole project. If you and your contractor have been talking to each other along the way, if mistakes have been worked out either through compromise, correction, or adjustment, and if you feel you have been treated fairly and honestly, compiling the punch list is a minor event, one that's even enjoyable. It gives you and your contractor a chance to review and admire the work that has been done and, almost incidentally, the opportunity to note and take care of the few minor glitches that will bring the project to perfection. This was the frame of mind we were in as we toured our project with our builder.

Contractor: *The builder usually has a list of things he knows about already. We do make mistakes, but a good contractor will correct his mistakes without ever being told about them.*

On the other hand, if the job has not gone smoothly, if you feel you have been taken advantage of, if you feel your contractor has been doing sloppy work, and if you have been bottling up your feelings and frustrations, you will be tempted to use the punch list as a weapon to make your contractor really earn his final payment.

Homeowner: *At the beginning of our project, we wanted to get along with our GC, we wanted to trust him, so we let little mistakes slide by for the sake of peace, until we finally realized a lot of things were not right. By the time we got to the end and were making out the punch list, we had become overly critical because we had let all those little things add up.*

Who Makes Out the Punch List?

You will certainly want to take notes about details that aren't quite right as the job winds down, but your GC should be the one who prepares the punch list—with your input. The punch list usually is drawn up during a formal inspection of the project by the GC, the architect (if you have one), and you. The GC is the person who is ultimately responsible for clearing up the problems on the list, and he should have a voice in determining what deserves to be on the list, since resolving these problems is the final step in his fulfilling the contract. He shouldn't be held responsible for work done by people you may have hired or products you bought.

Design/Remodeler: *I believe the contractor should be keeping a punch list, and the home-owner shouldn't have to concern himself with it. A good contractor has good quality control and catches the mistakes himself. Ideally you should have faith that your contractor is keeping such a list, because you can get him mad if you start pestering him about things before the job is over. Give your contractor a chance to finish the job and to ask you if there is anything you think he's missed. Unless you want to declare war, don't ask your lawyer to send him a list of twenty-five items with a note saying the final payment will be made when these are all done.*

What Qualifies for the Punch List?

The punch list is usually made up of small items, like "install locks on windows," "touch up paint in bedroom," or "replace trim over the living-room window." This is also the place to list the items that have not been installed or are back-ordered from the manufacturer, items the contractor will have to install eventually, such as the hardware for the kitchen cabinets or, as in our case, the new living-room windows.

One interesting category of punch-list items came up recently when a homeowner told me about finding that his front door bell had been disconnected and all the wires removed during construction. When he mentioned it to the contractor, he was told that installing a doorbell was not in the contract. "Of course it wasn't in the contract. Why would I ask for something I already had?" the homeowner said. He didn't get a new doorbell.

What Doesn't Belong on a Punch List?

There are some items that don't belong on a punch list. You should be prepared to accept these as your responsibility, like the oak cabinet doors that you removed and stored in the damp basement, where they became slightly warped. Your builder will not rebuild them. There are also some basic tasks like a new roof or a foundation that are either done or not done. They don't really belong on a punch list.

Punch-list items are more likely to crop up in finish work and detail work. These are the things you will notice first, but you should not demand unreasonable perfection. If the natural wood trim the carpenter installed doesn't quite match the original wood next to it, you're out of luck. It's very difficult to match eighty years of polishing and aging with a couple of coats of stain and lacquer.

Other items you can't put on the punch list are malfunctioning appliances or light fix-tures you went out and bought on your own and had the contractor install. He may have put the dishwasher in for you, but if its timer doesn't work, that's not his responsibility to take care of—it's yours.

The punch list is a one-shot process. There may be some items that will take time to correct or deliver, but you can't continue to add items to the list as you live in the space. Except for some basic structural members that your contractor guarantees for a year, this is your home, and you are going to have to accept the responsibility for doing your own maintenance work.

Contractor: *Many homeowners will have a second and third list waiting for the contractor when he finishes the first and comes back to be paid. Eventually he will get ticked off and walk off the job because what's left in the job is not worth the time and frustration to put up with this.*

How Builders Handle a Punch List

Homeowner: *Grudgingly, slowly, or not at all.*

Many contractors hold completing the punch list in much the same regard as having a tooth pulled or paying income taxes. But your contractor also knows that his contract with you specifies that those last-minute details have to be taken care of if he's to get his final payment.

Because the GC is responsible for the entire job, any punch-list items caused by one or more of his subcontractors are his problem. Sometimes he may do little repairs himself and back-charge the sub. If a problem is major, he will get the sub to come back and fulfill his obligations.

Some contractors keep a man on their crew who specializes in taking care of punch-list items. This is usually someone who is a pretty good carpenter but can also handle a paint brush, change a light switch, install a plumbing fixture, replace a cracked window, and soothe a disgruntled homeowner.

In our case it was the contractor himself who combined all those abilities and did the work. He hooked up the spray hose in the kitchen sink, planed a couple of doors that stuck, even ran an extra length of gutter around a corner and put on a new downspout so our deck looked neater.

Homeowners' Experiences with Punch Lists

When I asked homeowners I interviewed about their builder's punch-list performance, I got two completely different reactions. A look of resignation would come over the faces of many, and they would proceed to recount long stories of frustration and nonperformance. The remainder simply reported it as the final step in the process and no big deal. The punch list seems to be like a final exam. If you have been keeping up on the homework, you can take the test in stride. But if you have been letting things slide and have to cram everything into the last couple of nights, it can be a nightmare.

Homeowner: *Correcting items on the punch list was not my builder's strongest point. Because he had gone on to his next job, I had to call him several times. He finally got back to us and everything turned out okay, but I had to nag him. It wasn't that he didn't care—he came back to check out the kitchen several months after it was done to see if everything was okay—he just didn't have the time.*

It is at the punch-list stage that many contract misunderstandings first come to light. The homeowner assumes something is considered part of the job. The contractor assumes it is not. One homeowner's problems went on long after the actual remodeling was done.

Homeowner: *Our contractor didn't rebuild the outside stone steps after he built the addition on our house. At first he claimed it was not part of the agreement. Then, about a month later, he came back while we were away and put in a completely different set of steps made out of small stones. Then he wanted us to pay him extra. He finally did the steps over the way we wanted them, mainly because we had not paid the final amount, and he had to do it to our satisfaction to get paid.*

In a few instances, creating a punch list and trying to get your contractor to do anything about it will be a complete waste of time.

Homeowner: *We drew up a very detailed, very legaleze punch list for our New York contractor and got the bastard to sign it—it didn't mean a thing. He walked away from it. Actually, the contractor had underbid the job by quite a lot, and we all knew he would lose even more money if he completed all the loose ends.*

A Rational Approach
to the Final Payment

You can't expect to keep all your money in the bank until the last nail is driven and the last molding painted and then write one check to cover it all. The contract will clearly stipulate at what points in a project you will be expected to pay for the work done to date, but as the project approaches the "final payment," there is often no clear-cut understanding of what the contractor has to do to end the job and get paid so tensions mount. This is a difficult period for both you and your contractor. Your project is essentially done, and your contractor wants to get paid and move on to the next project, which he has probably started already. He doesn't want the last payment due him to be held up for a twenty-dollar part, or while you nitpick him to death. You want to get back to a normal way of life but are afraid that if you release that final payment, the contractor will disappear, and all those little items on the punch list will remain undone and an irritation for years to come.

You can both find plenty of historical evidence to support your concerns. Fortunately, there are ways to break this deadlock. You can specify in your contract that you'll hold back your final payment for a certain number of days—between ten and sixty days, depending on who wins the discussion while writing the contract. During this period your contractor can create the punch list, and, when all the items are taken care of, you can issue the final payment.

If, by the end of the time period, your contractor still hasn't completed a few items, or you're waiting for a part to be delivered, retain an amount sufficient to cover that item or part plus the cost of its installation, and release the remainder to your contractor. It really isn't fair to hold up 15 percent of the cost of a project until the knobs for the kitchen cabinets arrive.

What If You and Your Contractor Can't Agree?

You and your contractor can reach an impasse anywhere along the line, but it's usually as the job is winding down that a situation comes up that the two of you simply can't agree on. All it takes is for you to request what you think is a small change and for your contractor to fail to explain how much that "small" change will cost or to do much more work than you requested. But the damage is done. You refuse to pay for it. You're at an impasse.

There are several options open to you. One of you can give in, both of you can calm down enough to work out a compromise, you can take the problem to arbitration, or you can continue to scream and yell at each other until one of you gets mad enough to call in a lawyer.

Giving In

Giving in is not an unreasonable approach to keeping the peace. It is a tactic most often used in the early phases of a project, like the homeowner accepting the $2,000 increase to the foundation estimate. It is also a tactic that wears thin if exercised too often. Once the homeowner feels taken advantage of, he or she will resist all further negotiation even on comparatively minor items.

Calming down and Working out a Compromise

The best approach is to keep talking, try to understand each other's point of view, and work out a solution that is fair to both or even a little unfair to both. This approach (and the previous one) are applicable only if the contractor involved is ethical and honest. If for some reason you decided to go with a fly-by-night outfit, you might as well start protecting your interests early by lining up an arbitrator or your attorney.

Going to Arbitration

In most states all remodeling contracts call for an arbitration clause. It's a good idea for both parties. Going to court is expensive, time-consuming, and rarely satisfactory. The arbitration route is fairly simple and gives you and your contractor a chance to sit down in an informal setting and tell your respective sides of the story. There are no attorneys, no jury, no complicated proceedings or procedures, and you usually get a ruling within a couple of days rather than the months involved in a court trial.

Where to find arbitrators. The procedures for requesting an arbitration hearing will vary from state to state, but you can usually find an arbitrator through your state's contractor's or builder's board. Or you can seek assistance from your state's attorney general's office, the Better Business Bureau, or the Chamber of Commerce. The American Arbitration Association and a surprising number of other groups can also provide arbitrators.

Binding or nonbinding arbitration. Your contract should specify which form of the two arbitration systems you will agree to. My recommendation is to go with binding arbitration, which means you each agree that the arbitrator's decision is final. Get the thing over with and get back to work.

Wrapping Up Details

Before you make out that last check, there are some things you should get from your contractor:

Lien Releases

The contractor should provide a signed release form from each subcontractor and supplier he has used on your project. The forms will confirm that each has been paid for the materials and labor in full by the contractor and that they relinquish all rights to filing liens against your property.

The Certificate of Occupancy

If yours has been a substantial remodel, and especially if you have added new rooms, you may need a final inspection by the local building inspector, during which he or she will determine if you and your contractor have complied with all the building requirements of the community. Your contractor should arrange for this inspection and certificate at the point in the construction when all work is "substantially complete." In our case the local building inspector declared our project to be substantially complete even though the painters were still painting, the finish carpenter was still working on the kitchen cabinets, and several doors still had to be hung. But the house's basic systems (heating, electrical, and plumbing) were completely installed and working. If you have been living outside your home, you can only move back in once you have that certificate of occupancy.

Warranties

If you have had a new kitchen, a heating system, a hot tub, or even certain building components installed, there may be individual manufacturers' warranties on these appliances and products. Your contractor should turn the registration forms over to you, along with any maintenance or operating instruction booklets. (These frequently get tossed out with the packing cases they come in, so alert the contractor to the fact you want them.)

The date that your project is declared "substantially complete" marks the start date for all warranties except those items listed on your punch list. Those warranties will start the day you make your final payment.

Receipts

Your contractor should have attached receipts for all the materials he has purchased, his subcontractor's bills, and copies of the time cards for his crew to the bills he submits to you for payment. If you haven't gotten them from the very beginning, ask your contractor to supply them. Even if you can't make head or tail of them now, eventually you will need those receipts when you sell your house to reduce the taxes you will have to pay on the difference between what you originally paid for the house and the selling price.

You won't be in any shape mentally to create a detailed filing system during or immediately after a remodeling project, so I recommend you use our system: Get a box from your liquor store, label it *house stuff,* and put everything in it. In go those preliminary sketches you made, all the changes, the magazine pages you tore out, and finally, the contract, change orders, meeting notes, and sales receipts. Yes, it will be a mess, but it narrows down the search area considerably when you have to find something.

Callbacks

What do you do when three months after your job is finished a crack appears in a wall, a bedroom door won't close any more, or the double-hung window in the living room won't open? You call your contractor and demand that he fix it.

He would like to ignore you, and sometimes he does. He knows these things are not really his fault, but there is a clause in the standard contract, written or implied, that says he guarantees his work for one year.

A *callback* is the dread of any builder. If the punch list is a toothache, callbacks are a lobotomy without anesthetic. It is in the nature of construction with wood that things will move and shift as the seasons progress. That's especially true in the Northeast, where your home makes huge swings from summer dampness to winter aridity, thanks to central heating. These wide swings in humidity can raise havoc with wood paneling and behind the walls of your house.

Let me tell you a story to illustrate this point. When our remodel was complete, one of the first things I built in my new woodworking shop was a pine cabinet for my dart board. When I hung it on the door of my office in August, the cabinet doors barely closed. It was a beautiful fit. By the middle of December, the dryness had made both of the 10-inch boards split from top to bottom, and there was a ½-inch gap between the doors. By the following summer everything had come back together.

A similar sort of shifting is going on behind the walls of your house. It's not entirely fair to blame your builder because, as many builders have told me, the quality of the lumber available from lumberyards has deteriorated in recent years. Kiln-dried lumber has a water content much higher than used to be acceptable, and even the grading system for lumber has slipped several notches. While every competent builder allows for some shrinkage and movement, it's not possible to anticipate the wide range of movement that can take place. Hairline cracks in wallboard or plaster walls are not uncommon and are usually beyond the control and responsibility of your contractor.

How Builders Handle Callbacks

Because wood isn't static, there are some things your builder can't do much about. That hairline crack in the wall could have been caused by wood shrinking or by your new foundation settling or heaving a bit. The best you can expect him to do is to spackle the crack and paint it.

Since he is well aware of the characteristics of wood, your builder usually will accept responsibility for sticking doors, cabinets, and windows because his crew should have allowed for that movement when they installed them.

Design/Remodeler: *If we are coming into the humid summer season and a former client calls about a door sticking, I'll try to put her off until later. I know if one cupboard door is sticking now, more will be sticking later, and my guys will have to make several trips. I suggest living in a house for a while and letting the shelves and cabinets and drawers and doors do their initial shifting, and then asking us to come in and adjust everything at once.*

Remember that your contractor has doubtless moved on to the next job, which is probably just as complicated as yours was.

Contractor: *Understand that your contractor can't drop everything and come to you. If he comes over within a week to check it out and within a month to correct it, if he feels it is his responsibility, consider that good service because he is probably in the middle of another project in which the people are as unreasonable as you were.*

Contractor: *Tell us if it is an emergency. If it is, we will come immediately, but if it isn't, let us work it into our schedule.*

Understand that this is a free service you are requesting, so be pleasant to your builder when you call him back. You may be pleasantly surprised.

Design/Remodeler: *I find that callbacks are a chance to shine because most builders will not do them. If you do them cheerfully and well, you make a very good impression, and frequently the clients will think of something else they want done or that a friend wants done, and you get some additional business.*

Now That You're Done...

As you bubble idly in your new Jacuzzi, cradle a steaming mug of coffee in your new kitchen, or crank up the World Series in your new den, take a moment to congratulate yourself on a job well done. Think of all the things you've learned since that first day when you decided, "It's time we got started." You and your spouse have discovered talents you probably didn't know you had in planning, decorating, decision making, human relations, and problem solving. You've learned to function as a team and may even have developed a new level of respect for each other's abilities. You have weathered a very difficult storm and deserve to enjoy some smooth sailing in your new quarters.

Now you can invite all those friends and neighbors who watched both the destruction and the construction process to come in and see what you've been doing. As you take them on the grand tour, you'll have a humorous story for every room, every fixture, every board, every tile. They may not have seemed like humorous incidents at the time, but the project's done now, it looks great, and there's nothing like knowing that no one is going to wake you up at dawn with a skill saw to improve your outlook on life. And since reading this book allowed you to approach this, your first remodeling project, as though it were your second, maybe you should tackle a second project as if it were your third. It would be a shame to waste all that hard-won knowledge and experience.

As you daydream and start to plan that next project, remember:

The Ten Commandments of Remodeling

Thou Shalt:

1. Spend the money and time to plan thoroughly.
2. Take the time to find skilled, honest craftspeople, get recommendations, check their references, and check their work.
3. Make sure everyone is bidding on the same plans and specifications.
4. Regard the low bidder with suspicion and negotiate.
5. Make sure you have a clear, strong, fair contract.
6. Develop a workable decision-making process with your spouse.
7. Visit the site every day and be available for decisions.
8. Talk to your contractor regularly and work out misunderstandings.
9. Pay your bills on time.
10. Keep your sense of humor.

Index

W

Guy Capelle
Noëlle Gidon

REFLETS
Méthode de français **1**

CAHIER
D'EXERCICES

HACHETTE
Français langue étrangère

http://www.fle.hachette-livre.fr

Couverture : Sophie Fournier.
Conception graphique et réalisation : Sophie Fournier.
Secrétariat d'édition : Claire Dupuis.
Illustration : Bernard Villiot.
Recherche iconographique : Any-Claude Médioni.

ISBN : 2 01 1551 17 X